# Stencils and Stencilling

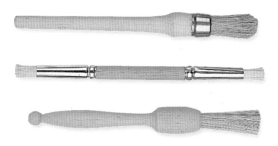

## Paula & Peter Knott

Haynes
THE BOOK ®

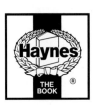

# Contents

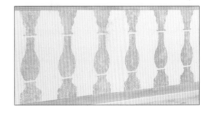

# Introduction

We have produced this book to give you all the information you need to be able to stencil a huge range of surfaces.

Stencilling can simply highlight a corner or decorate a favourite object, or it can create an all-embracing effect as a floor design or a complete wall scene. In 'Ideas and Choices' we aim to help you choose the right effect and subject for your project.

You probably have most of the equipment necessary. In 'Tools and Materials' we also include some that are specific to stencilling and give you tips on looking after your equipment.

Stencils need to be positioned accurately and the paint applied in the best way for the specific job in hand. In 'Basic Techniques' we cover the fundamental skills you need for any application.

Stencils can be applied to almost any surface in the home. In 'Surfaces to Stencil' we cover suitable paints and applications for decorating walls, doors, floors, furniture, fabrics and tiles, and in 'Projects' we take you through the decoration of a range of specific items from roller blinds to cakes!

'Illusions' gives ideas and practical solutions to show how you can transform a room using brushes or a sponge and stencils. Finally, the scope of designs becomes almost limitless when you make and cut your own stencils and it is surprisingly easy. We show you how in 'Designing and Cutting Stencils'.

We hope we will inspire you – happy stencilling!

# Ideas and Choices

Choosing a room to stencil, the surfaces to decorate, picking a design and working out a colour scheme provide you with a baffling number of options. Here inspiration is offered, with a range of rooms and surfaces to help you enjoy deciding your own schemes. In some cases designs are picked from textiles in the room, some use a range of stencils around a theme, others pick part of a design to use elsewhere in the room and others still add humour with illusions. And it is not just to the inside of the house that stencils add decoration. Use them to embellish a summer house or cheer up the garden shed.

# For the bedroom

Stencil designs can be picked from a bedding or curtain pattern to create an integrated theme. They can be positioned, high or low, on the walls to change the apparent shape of the room or used as a border to show off a pretty window, decorative bedhead or piece of furniture. By using a single topic but mixing stencil shapes, the walls of a child's bedroom can highlight a favourite pastime. When interests change it is simple to bring the design up to date by painting out some areas, using the base colour, and adding new shapes.

▼ Cupboard panels, decorated with flower-design stencils, appear more striking because not every panel has been filled.

▶ A space bordered by beams forms an ideal spot for a single stencil. The design is taken from the curtain fabric.

▲ Scaled up from the curtain fabric, a bold geometric design is used for a wall border that echoes the colours in the fabric.

◀ Stencils are easy to alter. The fairies here can be painted out, ready for new shapes to be added.

▶ A range of designs with similar subject matter can form an exciting mural like the scene depicted here.

▶ Your own designs mean any picture can be shown – such as a favourite rugby team.

▲ The rough surface of woodchip paper above the picture rail made the use of a bold stencil necessary here. The bed linen was the inspiration.

▲ Coir matting gains immediate interest with a broad stencilled frieze. Muted shades are produced by a final light spray of a soft sand colour.

# In the kitchen or bathroom

Most kitchens and bathrooms include large areas of hard, single-colour surfaces so stencils provide a wonderful, decorative contrast. Pattern can be introduced around windows, on walls, floors, tiles, fabrics and accessories. Seaside or other water themes turn bathtime into a sensuous pleasure for all age groups, while gastronomic delights, fruit, fish or fowl are ideal for a keen cook's kitchen. To protect stencils in these steamy areas, cover the finished designs with varnish.

◀ The glazed fruit design tiles on the wall and the china were the inspiration for the fruit frieze above the kitchen units.

◀ Ivy replaces a pelmet to border this window top, and a single stencil fills the front of the cooker hood.

▲ Stencils which are applied to dark-colour backgrounds must first be painted in white. This is what gives vibrance to the flowers on these kitchen cupboards.

◀ A range of seaside stencils is brought together to create an underwater world to enthuse anyone with the idea of bathtime.

▼ Even a plain shower curtain gains decorative effect with a stencilled design in colours that complement the room scheme.

◀ Stencilled themes create co-ordination on the walls, floor and container in this bathroom corner.

▶ A crossed cutlery symbol cleverly forms a sign above the hatch through to the kitchen.

# On almost any surface

The range of suitable paints for stencilling allows you to decorate a surprisingly wide choice of surfaces. Apart from interior walls, floors, furniture, fabrics and tiles, take stencils into the conservatory to add exotic plant species that never suffer from over- or under-watering or disease. Use stencils outdoors, too, where they can transform garden walls, fences and furniture. An old summer house or shed can be hidden or highlighted with a garden theme, or use a visual label to stencil a garden pot with a picture of the plant it contains.

◄ The summer house balustrading was created with nothing but stencils, masking tape, three colours of paint and a sponge.

▲ Any room can look like a conservatory with extra potted plants where stencils are used.

◄ An old potting shed is transformed by a lion's head.

► Fruiting and flowering lemon trees adorn this conservatory.

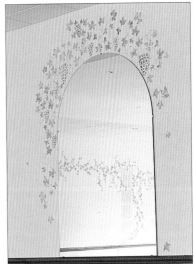

▲ The curved shape of a hall mirror is enhanced by a delicate frame of grapes used asymmetrically to echo nature. The stencilled walls opposite are highlighted in the mirror.

◀ A mock stone balustrade and ivy transform a summer house, granting views from every direction.

▲ A stone canopy design above this modern door turns an insignificant entrance way into an imposing feature.

▶ This modern cupboard could be mistaken for an antique with dark colours and a folk art design decorating it.

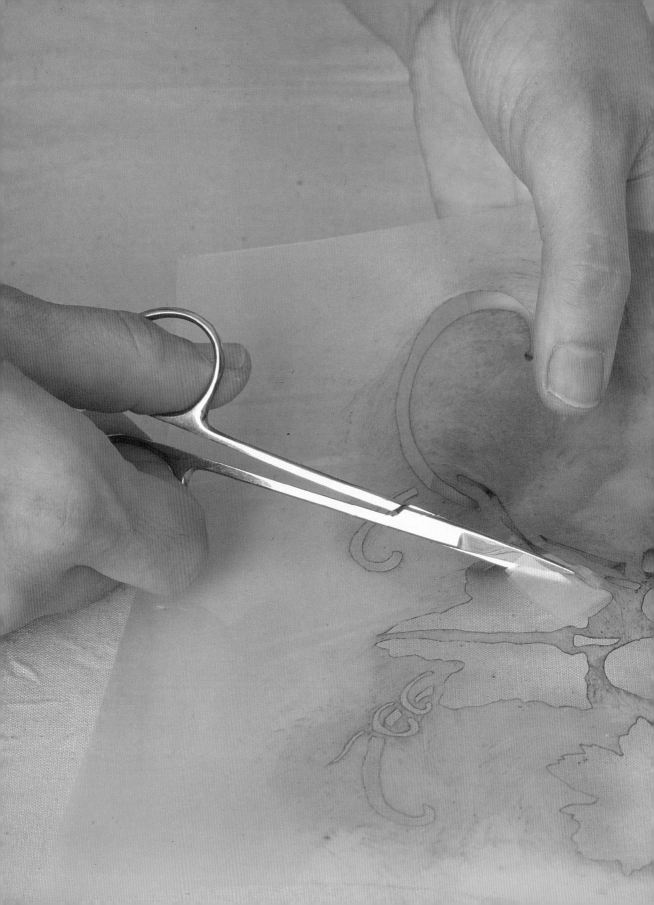

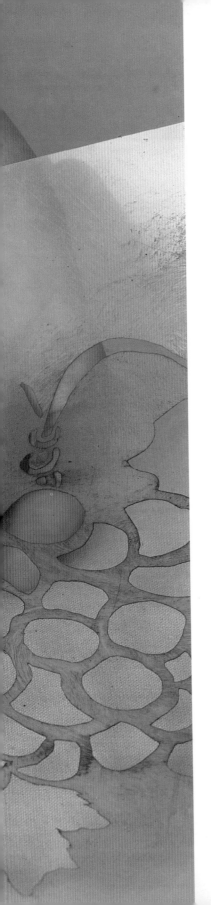

# Tools and Materials

Buy the best quality tools and materials you can afford. If you look after them carefully – cleaning them immediately after use, repairing them when necessary and storing them well – they will last a lifetime. Good tools make it much simpler to produce good results. Few tools and materials are unique to stencilling – you probably already have a number of the items listed in this chapter. Most of the general tools and equipment shown are available from stationers, decorating shops and DIY stores. Other less commonly used items can be obtained from art and graphic design materials suppliers and from craft shops.

# Types of stencil

There are three main types of stencil: single layer stencils; multiple layer stencils; and detailing stencils. On single layer stencils the complete design, including any detail, appears on one sheet. Multiple layer stencils usually comprise a separate layer for each colour appearing in the stencil, while detailing stencils add intricate shapes to a simple stencil design. A single layer stencil is the quickest to use, a multiple layer stencil is the simplest to use but takes more time as each colour is applied using a different stencil. A detailing stencil is the most complicated to design but produces the most sophisticated and elaborate results. Manufactured stencils are available in five materials and four of these materials are also available as sheets for designing and making your own stencils.

## STENCIL TYPES

### Single layer stencils

All the colours are applied using one stencil. Although care has to be taken to use the correct colours and cut-outs, colours can intermingle to great effect. The 'bridges' are unique to this method. Most of the designs given in this book use a single layer stencil.

### Multiple layer stencils

A separate stencil is made for each colour so they do not intermingle. Multiple layer stencilling is time consuming and the stencils need to be taped in place with care. The lack of colour gradation, unless you add tones or highlights (see step 4, page 31) means the result can appear flat and stark.

### Detailing stencils

In this technique a single layer stencil is used for the main outlines, then detail is added with one or more stencils using either different colours, or a different intensity of the same colour. Detailing stencils provide much more intricate shapes than would otherwise be possible.

## MATERIALS FOR MAKING STENCILS

### Clear acetate

A thin plastic sheet material with some of the advantages of transparent polyester, but it can stretch. If cut to a sharp point it can rip, and with use it becomes brittle. It is thus only suitable for use a few times.

### Oiled stencil card

Together with brass, oiled stencil card is the traditional material for stencils. The card, which has been steeped in linseed oil, is fairly pliable and is, to some extent, waterproof. It is not transparent, so a design must be transferred onto it rather than being applied directly to the surface. However, it is fairly hard wearing and easy to use.

### Transparent polyester

This strong sheet material is see-through, so a design can be drawn directly onto it, allowing you to see the surface beneath. It is easy to use and durable.

### Draughting film

A cheaper form of tracing paper, this is easy to cut. But it is not durable and should only be used for small one-off designs.

### Brass

Used for some manufactured stencils, it is tough but difficult to use because it is inflexible. If bent it is unusable, as the stencil will not lie flat on the surface behind, causing colour bleeding.

## COMPARING STENCIL MATERIALS

| MATERIAL | COST | READILY AVAILABLE | DURABLE | CUTTING METHOD | ABLE TO BE CLEANED | FLEXIBLE | WATER-PROOF | LASTING PERIOD FOR MATERIAL |
|---|---|---|---|---|---|---|---|---|
| Oiled card | Cheap | Yes | Fair | Scalpel | No | No | Fairly | 40–50 uses |
| Draughting film | Cheap | Yes | No | Scalpel | No | Yes | Fairly | 40–50 uses |
| Brass | Expensive | No | Yes | Pre-cut | Yes | No | Yes | 100+ uses |
| Transparent acetate | Cheap | Yes | Fair | Scalpel Hot knife cut | Yes | Yes | Yes | 100+ uses |
| Transparent polyester | Cheap | Yes | Yes | Scalpel Hot knife cut | Yes | Yes | Yes | 300+ uses |

# Stencilling equipment

A stencil needs securing well to the surface to be decorated if clear, sharp-edged results are to be obtained. It also needs to be easy to remove and reposition for further stencilling without marking or damaging the surface. Luckily there are excellent materials available for this. If you intend designing and cutting your own stencils, some specialist equipment makes the job much easier and more proficient. You will also need a number of commonly used decorating materials to make the job of stencilling run smoothly.

## FOR FIXING A STENCIL TO A SURFACE

**Masking tape**
Used to attach a stencil to a surface. Low tack tape is the best, or de-tack it yourself (see step 5, page 29).

**Re-positioning spray adhesive**
Applied to the back of a stencil to hold it securely in place. The stencil can be removed easily and reapplied elsewhere. Available from art and graphic supply shops.

**CAUTION**
Always follow manufacturer's instructions on the can when using spray adhesive. It should not be inhaled, so wear a mask and work in a well-ventilated area. Avoid contact with eyes or skin. It is also highly inflammable: keep away from heat, do not smoke while using it and when empty, dispose of it safely. Store well out of the reach of children.

## FOR MAKING AND CUTTING STENCILS

**Solvent-based permanent pen**
Ink from this pen cannot be smudged and it is therefore ideal for drawing out a stencil design on transparent plastic materials (see pages 16–17).

**Craft knife**
A slim-style craft knife is best. Its sharp blade ensures accuracy and a smooth line, but it takes skill and control to use the knife. Use with a resealable cutting mat. Best method for cutting card.

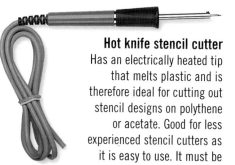

**Hot knife stencil cutter**
Has an electrically heated tip that melts plastic and is therefore ideal for cutting out stencil designs on polythene or acetate. Good for less experienced stencil cutters as it is easy to use. It must be used with a glass base.

**Glass**
Designs to be cut with a hot knife stencil cutter (left) should be placed over a sheet of plate glass before cutting. Either use polished-edge glass or bind the cut edges with masking tape.

### Cutting mat
A professional re-sealable cutting mat has a surface that reseals after running a knife across it, so it is worth the expense. The surface also helps to restrain the knife, preventing an over-cut.

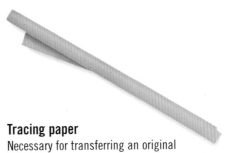

### Tracing paper
Necessary for transferring an original design onto stencil card. As it is waterproof, it can occasionally be used for cutting a stencil for a single use.

### Correction tape
This special tape is used to repair stencils as it is hard wearing. Available from good stationers.

---

## OTHER USEFUL TOOLS AND MATERIALS

### Step ladder
Essential for stencilling out-of-reach areas. When buying a step ladder, choose one with a platform on which to hold the palette while you are working, and with a handle, for safety. When working on a high wall border, use two step ladders with a plank between them.

**SAFETY NOTE**
Make sure that a step ladder is secure and on an even surface before climbing up it. Adjust the ladder if necessary.

### Absorbent kitchen paper
Useful for removing excess paint from the brush.

### Chalk
Marks design position. Choose a colour not too different from the surface colour but which is easily seen. Wipe off later with a damp cloth. Or use a soft pencil and a rubber.

### Steel rule
Measures from a straight edge to the position for a single stencil border.

### Lining paper
Use as practice paper to try out a stencil design – repeating until satisfied; or to mask out around a stencil when spray paint is applied (see page 29).

### Palette or plate
Useful for holding and mixing colours. A buffet plate, in sections, is ideal.

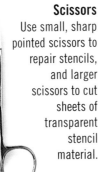

### Scissors
Use small, sharp pointed scissors to repair stencils, and larger scissors to cut sheets of transparent stencil material.

### Old cotton towel
Useful for drying damp brushes and wiping up spilt paint.

### Spirit level
Checks horizontal and vertical lines and ensures stencils are accurately aligned.

### Dust sheets
A range of dust sheets is useful for protecting the surfaces beneath an item being stencilled, or to protect against colour misting when using spray paints.

# Paint choices

Both water-based and oil-based paints can be used for stencilling but some paints are much more suitable for use over specific bases than others (see chart on pages 40–41). Also some paints take a long time to dry – you will work faster if you use acrylic, stencil, or spray paints or crayons. When using oil-based paints, clean tools and materials with white spirit. For water-based paints, see below.

## WATER–BASED PAINTS

### Acrylics
Acrylic paints come in a wide range of colours at a reasonable cost. They can dry too quickly, and need an extender to prolong the drying period. Available from art suppliers in a wide range of colours, they can also be mixed to obtain the required shade.

### Stencil paints
These are specially designed for stencilling. They are fast drying, high pigment, water-based paints. Use strong colours but apply a minimum of paint. Colours can be mixed.

### Fabric paints
Always use special fabric paints on fabrics which are going to be washed regularly. They are available from craft shops.

### Emulsion
Emulsion is not ideal because it takes too long to dry, restricting stencil repositioning. A long drying time can also cause bleeding beneath the stencil. For stencilling, use strong colours.

### AFTERCARE
Clear the sink area and use warm running water to wash all tools and materials. If the paint has dried, use a little detergent and soak to soften the paint. Then wash as above. For an ultra-clean brush, when you have washed out most of the paint, soak brush for a few hours in a carton of water, then rinse again. (See also page 24.)

## OIL–BASED PAINTS

### Ceramic paints
Designed for use on ceramic or glass surfaces, ceramic paints are also ideal for stencilling onto tiles. Cold-cure ceramic paints are best as they do not require firing in an oven afterwards.

### Artists' oils
Oils come in a wide range of colours, but are not ideal for stencilling as they can take in excess of two days to dry. They are available from art material suppliers.

### Spray paints
Aerosol spray paints, found in most car maintenance shops, come in a wide range of colours and can create a wonderfully subtle effect. However, they are not easy to use and require practice to obtain a good result. Please note the caution, below.

### Stencil crayons
Sticks of solid oil-based paint can be found in some art supply shops. The crayon is rubbed onto a palette and the paint picked up with a brush (see pages 32–33). There is a wide range of colours available, and you can also mix colours. However, some shades can fade with time.

### Gloss, eggshell and satin finish paints
Manufactured in a wide range of colours, they need a long drying time and are therefore only suitable for one-colour stencils.

### CAUTION
Always follow the manufacturer's instructions on the can when using spray paints. Wear a mask and work in a well-ventilated area – outside if possible. Avoid contact with eyes or skin. These paints are also highly inflammable: keep away from heat, do not smoke, dispose of cans safely. Store well out of the reach of children.

## VARNISHES

### Water-based varnish
This is ideal for protecting the finished work, as it is clear and does not yellow with age in the way oil-based varnish does. Apply it through the cut-outs of a stencil or over the complete surface.

### Oil-based varnish
Specially tough, oil-based varnish is best used to protect stencils which have been painted onto furniture or floors. (See also page 33.)

# Applicators

The only form of paint that does not require a separate applicator is aerosol spray paint. The most commonly used applicator for stencilling is a special brush with short, chopped-off bristles. A brush produces the best shaded effects; a sponge, which covers the surface quickly, is ideal for large areas and to mimic natural materials like stone, moss and grass. Whichever applicator you choose, use as little paint as possible, and go over the surface a number of times to build up colour gradually if a deeper colour or shading is required.

## STENCIL BRUSHES

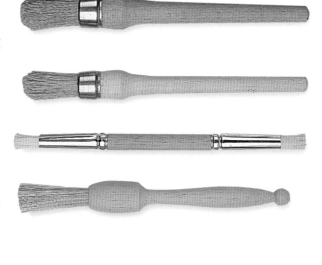

### ▶ Soft, domed brushes

Use with a swirling action or a stippling action (see Stencilling Techniques, page 31). This brush creates a soft effect and is quick and easy to use. The domed end of the brush can be pinched to a point for fine-detail shading. One brush does most jobs, although you will need a separate brush for each colour used.

### ▼ Stiff, flat-topped brushes

Use for stippling to give the results shown in Stencilling Techniques, page 31. Stippling is hard work and there is a temptation to speed up the work by applying too much paint at one time. The result is a blot on the wall (see pages 36–37). These brushes are not easy to control. You will need smaller size brushes for shading.

### DIY STENCIL BRUSH

If you are unable to purchase a stencil brush, a decorating brush, bound with masking tape, creates a good substitute. Use a small brush, less than 5cm (2in) wide, and bind about 2.5cm (1in) from the end of the bristles.

## SPONGES

Both natural and synthetic sponges can be used. A sponge is ideal for applying colour to large areas such as a floor or mock stone pillar. The paint should be slightly diluted so that the sponge does not become clogged. However, great care must be taken not to overload the sponge or bleeding will occur – remove excess paint before you start (see page 35).

### ▼ Natural sea sponge
This produces a soft, broken finish which is particularly effective in creating depth and texture when different colours are sponged on simultaneously.

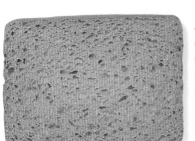

### ◄ Synthetic sponge
Colours can either be wiped over the surface or dabbed on, with a synthetic sponge.

## SPRAYERS

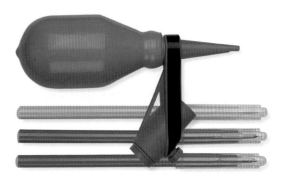

### Blitzer and aerosol spray
The stippled or dotty effect given by these applicators can be very attractive. However, both methods require practice. The blitzer uses air to blow the paint from the end of the felt tip, through the stencil, onto the surface. Great care must be taken to create an even result. For safe use of aerosol spray paints, see page 21.

## THE FINISHED EFFECTS OF DIFFERENT APPLICATORS

**Stiff brush**

**Soft brush**

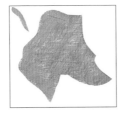

**Sponge**

**Blitzer**

**Aerosol spray**

# Caring for tools

Looking after your tools pays dividends. Wash brushes immediately after use, and clean stencils regularly to avoid clogging and ensure that a crisp result is produced. Narrow bridges in stencils can break in use or during cleaning – so clean with care. If they do break, they are easily repaired and it is best to do this straight away so that no extra pressure is put on the delicate surface while the stencil is in use.

*Cleaning and storing brushes*
**TOOLS:** Brush to be cleaned, hairdryer
**MATERIALS:** Water or white spirit, scrap of towelling, kitchen paper, elastic bands or string

*Cleaning a stencil*
**TOOLS:** Stencil to be cleaned, nylon abrasive kitchen pad
**MATERIALS:** Water or white spirit, spray adhesive solvent, absorbent kitchen paper, sheets of plastic

*Mending a stencil*
**TOOLS:** Torn stencil, scissors or craft knife.
**MATERIALS:** Correction tape

## CLEANING AND STORING BRUSHES

1 Immediately after finishing work, clean brushes used for water-based paint by rinsing them under warm, running water. Clean brushes used for oil-based paint with white spirit. Then towel dry the brush.

2 Bind a strip of paper towel around the bristles to keep them straight, and hold in place, with an elastic band or string. Leave in a warm place to dry completely, then store flat. This way brushes keep their shape.

### TO RE-USE A BRUSH IMMEDIATELY

After washing, towel dry the brush then finish off the drying process with a hairdryer. After final use, clean as steps 1 and 2 and store the brush with the bristles bound.

## CLEANING A STENCIL

1 Stencils need regular cleaning. If water-based paint has dried, first soak the stencil in warm water to soften the paint. Lay the stencil on a flat surface and rub gently with a dampened nylon abrasive pad and finally rinse. Clean off oil-based paint with white spirit as soon as possible.

2 The spray adhesive on the reverse may be removed with the solvent recommended by the manufacturer or with nail varnish remover. Alternatively try using washing up liquid solution and carefully scrub with a nylon abrasive pad as in step 1.

3 Dry the cleaned stencil with absorbent kitchen paper, then store laid flat between two sheets of plastic.

## BEFORE MAKING REPAIRS

Always clean a stencil before repairing it (spray paint is almost impossible to remove, but there is little build-up so you can leave the remaining colour). If a stencil tears while you are working with it, re-apply spray adhesive to the back, which may keep the pieces together allowing you to finish the job. Don't try this if you have just begun to stencil a repeated design over a large area. Instead, repair as in steps 1 and 2, right.

## REPAIRING A TORN STENCIL

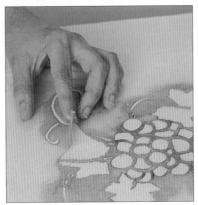

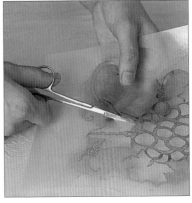

1 Breaks in a stencil can be repaired with correction tape (see pages 18–19). Apply a short length of tape to each side of the stencil, across the tear, to hold it in place securely.

2 Carefully cut excess tape away with a small pair of scissors, to leave the stencil design as it was before the damage. Alternatively use a craft knife to remove excess tape.

# Basic Techniques

Stencilling is an easily mastered skill that anyone can acquire with a little know-how. Once the basic techniques are learnt – marking position and fixing a stencil, applying paint and protecting the finished work – you are free to evolve your own designs and effects. Remember to remove any chalk marks you made when positioning the stencil, using a damp cloth. When stencilling onto a dark background, apply white stencil paint first.

Two people may start with the same stencil design and the same colour scheme, but the result each produces will be totally different. So, although stencilling is not difficult to do, the finished effect is unique to you. Don't be afraid of making mistakes, most are simple to rectify. And if you take time at the beginning to experiment on spare paper so that colours and technique can be perfected, then mistakes need never occur in the final result.

# Positioning stencils

Before starting stencilling check that the surface to be painted is in good decorative order. You also need to work out accurately where the design will go. On a large area, like a wall or floor, you will need to take measurements and draw in chalk lines to pinpoint positions. When you have done this, fix the stencil at the first point to be decorated. Remember to attach the stencil closely at the back to avoid seepage during stencilling. Later you will need to remove it without damaging the base surface.

(For safe use of spray adhesive see page 18.)

**TOOLS:** Chalk, metal rule, spirit level, stencil

**MATERIALS:** Re-positioning spray adhesive, masking tape, lining paper or newspaper, white spirit

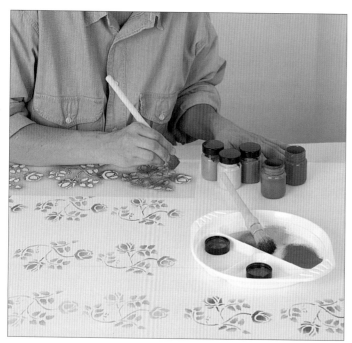

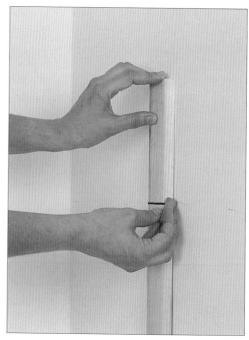

1 Ensure that the surface to be decorated is sound and no damage will result when the stencil is removed. Do a test sample on a similar surface to check which stencilling technique will work best (see charts, pages 40–41).

2 Work out the exact positions for the stencils. To do this use chalk and mark points to line up with the stencil edges, not the centre of the design.

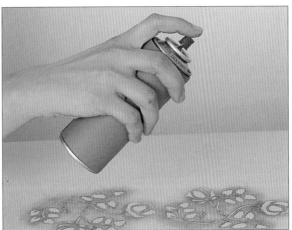

3 For a border design measure from the nearest parallel surface, ceiling, skirting, or dado rail, and mark at about 30cm (12in) intervals along the wall. Check with a spirit level that the marks you have made are level.

4 Place stencil on newspaper or paper, with the side to be painted face down. Hold the adhesive can about 20–30cm (8–12in) away from the surface and spray a mist of adhesive to cover the complete stencil back. Remove excess with white spirit.

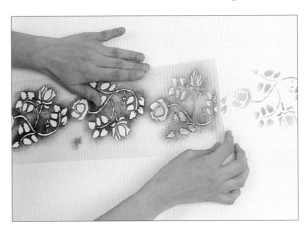

5 Detack any masking tape to be used by repeatedly sticking the tape onto a piece of fabric until you can see tiny 'hairs' on the back and it is less sticky. After use, remove the tape as soon as possible. Apply the stencil to the surface to be decorated. Add short strips of masking tape to the edges if necessary. Ensure that the stencil is straight and fixed securely. Stand back to check it visually, then rub your hand over the surface to make sure it adheres well.

## UNBLOCKING A SPRAY NOZZLE

If the nozzle on the can of adhesive spray becomes blocked, remove the nozzle and soak for at least 10 minutes in the solvent recommended by the manufacturer, or use nail varnish remover. Rub off excess adhesive, then use a pin to clean out the nozzle. Point the nozzle away from eyes.

## MASKING THE STENCIL

When using spray paint, a wide area surrounding the stencil needs to be protected to avoid colour misting. Mask an area of at least 30cm (12in) on all sides of the stencil. Use lining paper held with masking tape to cover the surrounding area.

# Using stencil paints

Once the stencil is in position you are ready to begin. Load the brush sparingly with paint and use one of the two main stencilling techniques, swirling or stippling, to apply it. Swirling creates a smooth, soft effect, stippling produces a dotted, textured finish.

You can combine the two techniques, or use one of the techniques to highlight texture. Put the paint on in very thin layers, using an almost dry brush, and the finish will soon acquire the cloudy, translucent quality which is characteristic of stencilling.

**TOOLS:** Stencil, stencil brushes

**MATERIALS:** Water-based stencil paints, palette (or old plate), scrap paper, newspaper

1 Assemble all the tools and materials. Shake the paint so that the inner lid is well coated and decant some paint from the lid onto the palette. Work with about one teaspoon at a time.

2 Dip the tip of the brush into the paint, without overloading it, and remove the surplus on a scrap of paper. Using too much paint can lead to paint bleeding under the stencil edges and give a heavy-looking result.

**3** Work the paint well into the bristles. To do this, swirl the paint on the brush onto a clean part of the palette. Do this between 5 and 30 times, until the brush feels tacky and nearly dry.

### STENCILLING TECHNIQUES

A circular, swift swirling action of the hand and brush gives a smooth effect which is quick to produce.

For a stippled effect, use a tapping action, dabbing evenly up and down all over the surface.

**4** Use either a circular or a stippling action to apply paint. Building up colour, where required, is done by applying more layers of paint. To shade a design, look at how light falls on natural objects or study tonal drawings. Use darker tones for areas in shade and white, or a paler shade of the original, for highlights.

### TEST BEFORE YOU START

It is very important to do a sample before decorating the surface to be stencilled. A length of lining paper makes a good sample sheet. Use this to perfect your technique and live with the sample for a few days so that you see it in both natural and artificial light. Adjust the colouring if necessary. Once you are satisfied with the result, you are ready to start.

**5** Once the design is complete, remove the stencil to inspect the result. If an area has been missed or some part needs extra shading, carefully replace the stencil to complete.

# Using stencil crayons

As an alternative to using water-based paints, oil-based stencil crayons can be used. These are solid sticks which, when rubbed onto a hard surface, soften, so that the paint may be picked up with a brush and treated as other paints.

The advantage of using these crayons is that it is almost impossible to put too much paint on the brush. The tough finish of oil-based paint makes these crayons ideal for use on shiny surfaces like tiles and surfaces which have been painted with oil-based paint.

Once a stencil is completed, if it will receive hard wear, such as on a floor or piece of furniture, you should coat your design with varnish to protect it.

(For safe use of spray adhesive see page 18.)

*Using stencil crayons*
**TOOLS:** Stencils, stencil brushes
**MATERIALS:** Spray adhesive, masking tape, oil-based stencil crayons, palette

*Protecting the work*
**TOOLS:** Stencil, household paintbrush or stencil brush
**MATERIALS:** Spray adhesive, masking tape, water or oil-based varnish

## STENCIL CRAYON TECHNIQUE

1 Apply spray adhesive to the stencil back, position and add masking tape (see pages 28–29). Remove the dry tip of the stencil crayon by rubbing it off onto spare paper. Rub the paint stick onto the palette. The creamy paint left behind is ready to use.

2 Pick up the paint on the brush by working the brush over the palette in swirls. Check that the paint is well distributed within the brush as this ensures that the painted result looks even.

**3** Use the swirling technique to produce a smooth, blended effect. If new colours are subsequently applied to the same area, these blend to produce a totally new overall colour.

**4** The use of stencil crayons produces an even finish. Colours blend rather than appearing separately and this gives less shading than other methods. Building up colour is difficult as you need to wait for the paint to dry between layers, and this can take hours to partially set, and days to go hard.

## PROTECTING YOUR WORK

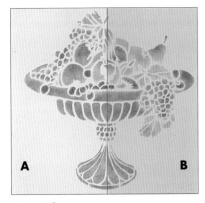

**Varnish**

Water-based varnish (**A**) is clear and easy to apply. Use over water-based paints – emulsion and acrylic. Polyurethane varnish (**B**) yellows with age – use over oil-based paints (gloss, eggshell and satin finish).

**Small areas**

If only the stencil design needs protection, or the surface around the design cannot be varnished, apply the varnish through the stencil by brushing it through the cut-out spaces.

**The complete surface**

Better protection is provided if the whole surface is varnished. Apply a thin coat of varnish for light protection, use two or three coats for a tough finish, allowing each coat to dry thoroughly.

# Stencilling large areas

Sponging using a marine or synthetic sponge, or spraying using aerosol spray paint, are the quickest methods of applying paint to large areas.

    When sponging, the paint needs to be slightly diluted and the sponge applied almost dry or bleeding may occur, leaving a smudged outline. When using the spray method, a wide area surrounding the stencil needs to be protected to avoid colour misting. Spraying needs some practice to obtain a result that is light and even. Do tests on spare paper to perfect your technique before you start on the surface to be decorated.

(For safe use of spray adhesive and aerosol spray paint, see pages 18 and 21.)

*Spray painting*
**TOOLS:** Stencil
**MATERIALS:** Spray adhesive, masking tape, aerosol spray paints, lining paper, dust sheets

*Stencilling with a sponge*
**TOOLS:** Stencil, natural sea sponge
**MATERIALS:** Spray adhesive, masking tape, glass jar, stencil paint, plate

## STENCILLING WITH SPRAY PAINT

1 Position the stencil, protecting the area around it with a mask (see pages 28–29). Start to spray from the edge of the stencil and move it across, using a light touch and moving the can all the time.

2 Apply fine subsequent layers of paint in the same way where you want to build up colour. Use either the same colour or new colours. As many as ten coats may be required for good coverage of any one area.

3 To add highlights, use yellow spray paint, to shade areas use a dark tone. Apply highlights and tones where light and shade would fall naturally (see step 4, page 31).

## STENCILLING USING A SPONGE

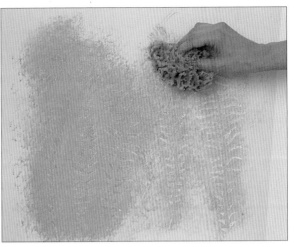

1 Attach the stencil (see pages 28–29). Dilute the paint with water in the glass jar. For strong colours use about 240ml (8fl oz) of water to 15ml (1tbs) paint. Work the paint well into the sponge and remove excess before you start stencilling.

2 Use a gentle dabbing action to apply the paint on the sponge to the surface. Join up the sponge shapes to form an overall, densely mottled effect.

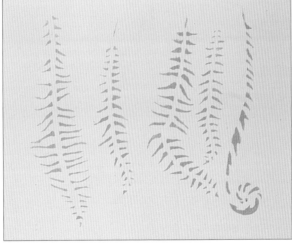

3 Use the second colour more lightly, so that the first colour still clearly shows. This second coat adds texture and depth. Extra colours may be used but are not usually necessary.

4 The finished stencil shows the texture produced by the sponge. Use this method to reproduce natural materials such as plants, sand, soil, grass and stone.

### SECURING LARGE STENCILS

Larger stencils may require the use of masking tape as well as spray adhesive to hold them securely in position.

Apply the tape in short strips at each corner and add extra strips at the top of the stencil if necessary. Remember to detack the masking tape and remove it as soon as possible or you may ruin your base surface (see step 5, page 29).

# Correcting mistakes

Everyone makes mistakes sometimes, but luckily most mistakes occur at the experimental stage. Ensure that you always do a sample on spare paper to iron out any problems before you start on the surface to be decorated. The most likely times you may make mistakes are when positioning the stencil and when applying the paint. Ensure that the stencil is securely fixed and accurately positioned, and use a minimum of paint and a soft brush.

## MISTAKES – HOW TO PREVENT AND CORRECT THEM

| PROBLEM | CAUSE | PREVENTION | SOLUTION |
| --- | --- | --- | --- |
| Paint seepage | Too much paint | Use less paint<br>Use spray adhesive | Dry stencil, paint out mistake |
| Stencilling too faint | Too little paint<br>Paint colour similar to base | Use more paint, or darker colour<br>Always do a sample first | Replace stencil and re-do |
| Design not straight | Chalk line not used or stencil itself is cut on the slant | Level should be used to check horizontals and verticals<br>Check stencil and re-cut edges | Paint out crooked section and re-do |
| Incorrect colour | Wrong colour on the brush | Check the colour on the brush | Replace stencil, use white or base colour to stencil it out, then re-do in correct colour |
| Colour too strong | Too much paint used<br>Colour of stencil paint too strong | Check colours against base before use<br>Always do a sample first | Replace stencil, use white or base colour to stencil it out, then re-do in correct colour |
| Second overlay incorrectly positioned | Stencil guide lines are incorrect<br>Poorly positioned | Do a sample before starting | Paint out the stencil and re-do |
| A background colour or pattern shows through | Surface stencilling does not obliterate the base colour or pattern | Stencil in white first. Allow to dry and re-stencil in the correct colours | Replace stencil, stencil in white and allow to dry, re-stencil in correct colours |
| Blurred edges | No spray adhesive used | Use spray adhesive | Paint out area and re-do |

## AVOIDING THE MOST OBVIOUS MISTAKES

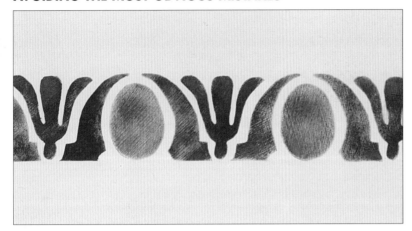

**1** Using a chalk line as a guide for the position of a stencil ensures that it is straight. A crooked design is usually the result of insufficient preparation in planning exactly where the design should go. Always follow the same procedure for positioning and fixing stencils (see pages 28–29).

**2** The crooked result shown cannot be corrected. To rectify the fault, paint this section out, draw in the guideline and repaint. Curling floral designs that are crooked can sometimes be disguised by re-positioning the stencil to add extra sections of the design at strategic points to help the overall appearance.

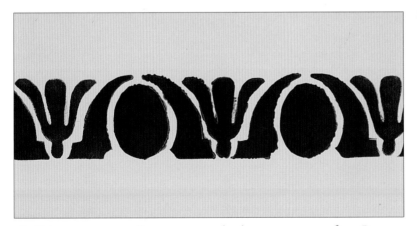

**3** Paint seepage usually occurs when a brush contains too much paint. Ensure that the brush is almost dry when you start – check on scrap paper first. Re-positioning with spray adhesive reduces the chance of seepage, as the stencil is stuck firmly.

**GETTING IT RIGHT**

If you are confident yet careful you are more likely to have success. If you make a mistake while working, continue until the job is finished, then stand back and check it is noticeable. At this point, if you decide the error needs correcting, rectify it by following the information in the chart on the left, Mistakes – How to Prevent and Correct Them.

# Surfaces to Stencil

Stencilled designs can be applied to most surfaces and are commonly used on walls, floors, furniture, fabrics and tiles. However, the paint used must be compatible with the surface, and in hard wear areas protected so that it does not wear off in use. On most fabrics, a washable fabric paint is advisable. On ceramics, tiles and glass, a ceramic paint is necessary.

Rough-textured surfaces may require a stippling, rather than swirling, action to apply the paint evenly. Some surfaces, such as terracotta or bare wood, can be stencilled with ordinary water-based stencil paints, but need varnishing to withstand wear and tear.

# Base surfaces

Although most paints will adhere to most surfaces, some are much more suitable for use than others. This chart not only shows the paints most suitable for use on a range of base surfaces, but the best methods of application, the type of stencil to use, how to fix it and the most suitable varnish to protect the end result.

## BASE SURFACES – PAINTS TO USE

| BASE SURFACE | WATER-BASED STENCIL | EMULSION | ACRYLIC | FABRIC | ARTISTS' OIL | CERAMIC | SATIN FINISH | SPRAY | CRAYON |
|---|---|---|---|---|---|---|---|---|---|
| Emulsion | • | • | • | • | • | | • | • | • |
| Satin finish | • | • | • | | • | | • | • | • |
| Gloss | | | | | • | | • | • | |
| Varnished bare wood | • | • | • | • | • | | • | • | |
| Sealed wood | • | • | • | | • | | • | • | |
| Melamine | • | • | • | | • | | • | • | • |
| Cotton | • | • | • | • | | | • | • | • |
| Silk | • | • | • | • | | | | • | • |
| Glass | | | | | | • | | • | |
| Ceramic/china | | | | | | • | | • | • |
| Tiles – gloss | | | | | | • | | • | • |
| Tiles – matt | | | | | | • | | • | • |
| Perspex | • | • | • | | • | | • | • | • |
| Terracotta | • | • | • | | • | | • | • | • |
| Textured wallpaper | • | • | • | • | • | | • | • | • |
| Blown vinyl | • | • | • | • | • | | • | • | • |
| Wood chip | • | • | • | • | • | | • | • | • |
| Bricks | • | • | • | • | • | | • | • | • |
| Grass | • | • | • | | | | | • | |
| Tongue and groove panel | • | • | • | • | • | | • | • | • |
| Cakes | *Use edible food colouring* | | | | | | | | |

## BASE SURFACES – METHODS TO USE

| BASE SURFACE | STENCIL RESTRICTIONS | HOW TO ATTACH STENCIL | APPLICATION METHOD | PROTECTION |
|---|---|---|---|---|
| Emulsion | None | Spray adhesive, masking tape | Brush/spray/sponge | Water-based varnish |
| Satin finish | None | Spray adhesive, masking tape | Brush/spray/sponge | Oil-based varnish |
| Gloss | None | Spray adhesive, masking tape | Brush/spray/sponge | Oil-based varnish |
| Varnished bare wood | None | Spray adhesive, masking tape | Brush/spray/sponge | Any varnish |
| Sealed wood | None | Spray adhesive, masking tape | Brush/spray/sponge | Any varnish |
| Melamine | None | Spray adhesive, masking tape | Brush/spray/sponge | Water-based varnish |
| Cotton | None | Spray adhesive, masking tape | Brush/spray/sponge | Iron to cure |
| Silk | None | Spray adhesive, masking tape | Brush | Cure as advised |
| Glass | None | Spray adhesive, masking tape | Brush/spray | Cure as advised |
| Ceramic/china | None | Spray adhesive, masking tape | Brush/spray | Cure as advised |
| Tiles – gloss | None | Spray adhesive, masking tape | Brush/spray | Cure as advised |
| Tiles – matt | None | Spray adhesive, masking tape | Brush/spray | Cure as advised |
| Perspex | None | Spray adhesive, masking tape | Brush/spray | Water-based varnish |
| Terracotta | None | Spray adhesive, masking tape | Brush/spray/sponge | Water-based varnish |
| Textured wallpaper | Large stencil, simple design | Spray adhesive, masking tape | Brush/spray | Water-based varnish |
| Blown vinyl | Large stencil, simple design | Spray adhesive, masking tape | Brush/spray/sponge | Water-based varnish |
| Wood chip | Large stencil, simple design | Spray adhesive, masking tape | Brush/spray/sponge | Water-based varnish |
| Bricks | Large stencil, simple design | Spray adhesive, masking tape | Brush/spray | Water-based varnish |
| Grass | Large stencil, simple design | Spray adhesive, masking tape | Brush/spray/sponge | None |
| Tongue and groove panel | None | Spray adhesive, masking tape | Brush/spray | Water-based varnish |
| Cakes | None | Sugar solution | Brush | None |

# Walls

When decorating walls first consider the style and use of the room. Take into account fabrics, carpets, wall texture, the period of the house and the atmosphere you want to create. Are you aiming for a smart, formal effect or a country cottage look? The style of the stencil and the colours used should take all these factors into account. Stencils can be applied to walls as a border design (see below), as a frieze (see pages 60–61), as a grouped arrangement (see pages 62–63) or as a complete wall design (see pages 80–81).

(For safe use of spray adhesive see page 18.)

**TOOLS:** Steel rule, spirit level, chalk, stencil, stencil brushes

**MATERIALS:** Spray adhesive, masking tape, water-based paint, palette

## USING A WALL BORDER

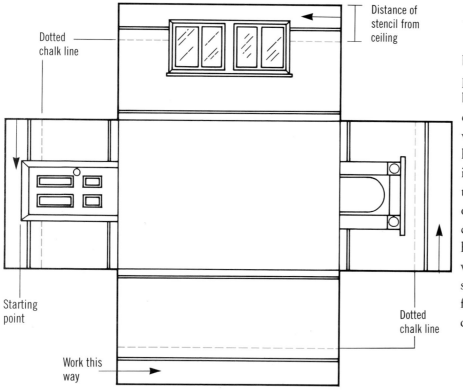

Dotted chalk line

Distance of stencil from ceiling

Starting point

Dotted chalk line

Work this way

1 First decide on the position for your border. Used at dado or picture rail level a border will lower the ceiling, so this works well in a room with a high ceiling. However, in a low-ceilinged room this effect could be overpowering. Borders can also be used to highlight a decorative window, show off a special piece of furniture, or edge a doorway.

2 Once you have decided on the position, chalk guide marks along the wall. Mark the position and prepare the stencil (see pages 28–29). Fix the stencil for the first application of paint in the least noticeable position, above a door, in an alcove or behind a large piece of furniture. You can then perfect your stencilling out of view. Apply paint to the stencil (see pages 30–35).

3 As you move along the wall, line up each stencil with your chalk marks. At a corner, gently tap the stencil into place on the wall you are working on, keeping the section on the other wall free. Stencil up to the corner, then position the remaining section of the stencil on the adjoining wall, peeling away the section you have just completed.

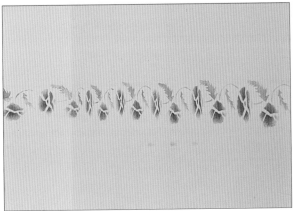

4 Due to the preparation work, each section of stencil lines up with the rest. Carefully remove any remaining chalk marks with a damp cloth.

## PLACING A BORDER

When using a narrow border consider placing it around both the top and bottom edges of the wall. You can also use a border to edge the ceiling in the same way that a plaster frieze often appears in older houses.

## TO MITRE A CORNER

On a border that surrounds a window or on a floor or piece of furniture, a mitred corner is often needed. Start stencilling at a corner. Draw a chalk line diagonally across the stencil design to create a mitre, then mask out all cut-out shapes beyond the drawn line. Stencil one side of the corner, then flip the stencil to paint the adjoining corner section. Repeat on the other corners.

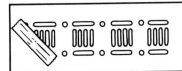

Mask the stencil as above at a corner, then flip it to turn the corner and produce the result illustrated on the left.

# Wall surfaces

Some stencilling methods are more suitable for use over specific wall surfaces than others. Rough or uneven wall surfaces also require simple, bold stencil designs for a satisfactory result. The chart below shows a range of wall textures and which stencilling method and stencil type is best used with each.

## STENCILLING TECHNIQUES TO USE

| SURFACE | STENCILLING METHOD | TYPE OF STENCIL TO USE |
| --- | --- | --- |
| Flat wall | Stipple, swirl or spray | Any |
| Textured wallpaper | Stipple or spray | Larger, simple designs |
| Tongue and groove panelling | Stipple or swirl | Larger simple designs |
| Concrete or brickwork | Stipple or spray | Larger simple designs |
| Textured wall | Stipple or spray | Larger simple designs |
| Terracotta | Stipple, swirl or spray | Any |

**Stencilling onto brickwork**

**Textured wallpaper**

**Textured wall**

# Doors

Doors receive more wear and tear than almost any other surface. The use of oil-based paint ensures that they are easy to clean and touch up. To stencil over an oil-based paint surface, a compatible and durable paint must be used. Paints such as satin finish oil-based paint, eggshell or gloss are compatible, and an aerosol car spray paint is equally hard-wearing. (For using spray paint see page 34.)

Stencilling can significantly change the look of a door, enhancing a panelled door or creating the effect of panels on a flat-faced flush door (see following pages).

(For safe use of spray adhesive see page 18.)

*Using oil-based paint*
**TOOLS:** Stencil, stencil brushes

**MATERIALS:** Satin finish oil-based paint, spray adhesive, palette

## USING OIL-BASED PAINT

1 Spray the back of the stencil with adhesive and fix the stencil in place on the door. (See also page 29.)

2 Apply satin finish oil-based paint with a brush (for technique see steps 2–3, pages 32–33). As so little paint is used, the paint dries in under 1 hour. If you need to reposition the stencil close to a wet area, wait until the first area is dry.

### COMPARISON WITH SPRAY PAINT

A comparison shows that, apart from the colours used, there is little difference in the result. Using satin finish paint on a small area takes less time because no masking is required.

# Panelling a flush door

You can form an apparently different style of door using a stencil design which creates the effect of a panel or panels. This may be embellished with motifs such as flowers, figures, heraldic symbols or animals to suit the style of room and its use. Adding tones and highlights (see step 4, page 31) will make the panelling more realistic.

Alternatively, add timber beading and stencil within and around this. If you use water-based paints for stencilling (see pages 40–41), two or three coats of varnish will provide a tough finish (see page 33).

(For safe use of spray adhesive and aerosol spray paints see page 18 and 21.)

*Panelling a flush door*
**TOOLS:** Stencil, stencil brushes

**MATERIALS:** Spray adhesive, oil-based stencil crayons, palette

## APPLYING A REPEAT PATTERN TO CREATE A CENTRE PANEL

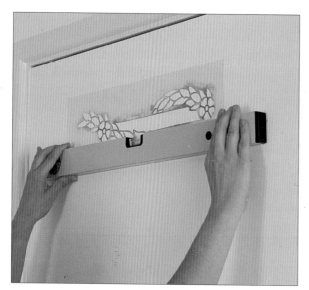

1 Measure the door and choose a stencil design which will create the effect of panels. Mark the stencil positions accurately and check the first position with a spirit level.

2 Spray the adhesive over the back of the stencil and position it carefully on the door (see pages 28–29). Use the brush to apply the paint to the stencil (see pages 32–33).

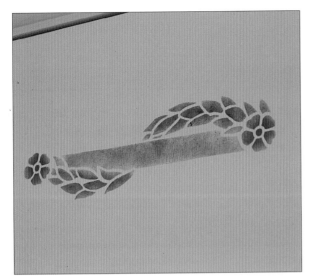

4 The design used here creates the effect of a central panel. If you decide to divide the door up into smaller panels, choose a smaller design. Other ideas are shown in the section, Ideas and Choices.

3 When painted, remove the stencil and check your work. When happy with the result, reposition the stencil and complete the panel. Mitre the corners if necessary (see page 43).

## PANELLING IDEAS

**Beaded border ▶**

Here timber beading, available ready mitred, has been fixed to a flush door to create panels. The stencilled star and moon create a focal point for each of the panels.

**Painted border ▶**

A painted border stripe creates a panelled edge to frame a central stencil design. To ensure straight lines when you are painting stripes, stick strips of detacked masking tape along either side of the stripe. Remove this as soon as painting is finished and before the paint has dried.

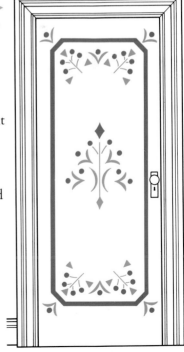

# Floors

A timber floor provides an ideal surface for stencilling and, once protected by several coats of varnish, becomes hard wearing and easy to clean. When planning a design bear in mind the positions of furniture and fittings, and always draw out the design first. Design ideas include a border, a striped or chequerboard design, a painted rug with tassels, stencilled shadows to give the impression of permanent sunshine or giant paw prints wandering through the room. Match up the patterns used on walls or furniture for a co-ordinated effect, or use different motifs incorporating the same theme.

*Floor border*
**TOOLS:** Stencils, stencil brushes, steel rule

**MATERIALS:** Spray adhesive, masking tape, water-based stencil paint, palette, water-based floor varnish

*Chequered floor design*
**TOOLS:** Fine grade sandpaper, stencils, sponge

**MATERIALS:** Water-based varnish, straight edge, chalk, spray adhesive, masking tape, water-based stencil paints, plate, floor grade polyurethane varnish

(For safe use of spray adhesive see page 18.)

## FLOOR BORDER

1 ▲ Work on a newly sanded floor if you can. In which case, apply a coat of water-based varnish to protect the surface. If the floor is already varnished or polished, clean the surface with a detergent, allow to dry and lightly sand it. Liberally spray the complete back of the stencils with adhesive so that they are held in close contact with the floor and arrange them carefully. Press down firmly.

2 Apply the paint (see pages 30–31). Use a nearly dry brush and build the paint up in thin layers. Do not obliterate the grain of the wood but allow it to show through the paint.

3 Once stencilling is complete, allow the last paint colour to dry and brush on three coats of water-based floor varnish. Remember to let the varnish dry thoroughly before applying subsequent coats.

**AGED LOOK**
For an aged look, leave the floor design without protection for a period. When natural wear has given it the finish you like, seal the area with varnish.

## CHEQUERED FLOOR DESIGN

1 Prepare the floor as in step 1, opposite. Work out the floor design and draw the outline on the floor before you begin, using a straight edge and chalk. Attach the stencil in the first position using spray adhesive.

2 Dilute the paint with equal parts of paint and water and work well into the sponge. Then apply the paint in a dabbing motion (see steps 1–2, page 35). Extra coats allow a denser finish but the effect looks best if the wood grain still shows through the finished design.

3 Once you have finished all of the stencilling, give the floor at least three coats of floor-quality varnish. It is best to maintain the surface by re-coating it with varnish about every six months or so.

# Furniture

Stencilling will help you add interest and colour to natural timber furniture, and you can disguise a poor surface by first painting it to match other items in the room. Large pieces of modern melamine-finish furniture can lose their overpowering effect if you paint them to match the walls. Mirror the room scheme or co-ordinate your stencil pattern with the design on curtains or furnishings as you prefer.

*Child's toy box*
**TOOLS:** Fine grade sandpaper, synthetic sponge, 2-part stencils, household paintbrush, fine grade wire wool

**MATERIALS:** Water-based stencil paint, spray adhesive, masking tape, palette, water-based varnish, wax polish

*Melamine cupboard*
**TOOLS:** Fine grade sandpaper, stencils, household paintbrush

**MATERIALS:** Emulsion or oil-based paint to match cupboard, spray adhesive, masking tape, water-based stencil paint, palette, water-based varnish

(For safe use of spray adhesive see page 18.)

## CHILD'S TOY BOX

1 Before colourwashing natural timber, sand the surface to provide a key. Make up colourwash with stencil paint, thinned 1 part stencil paint to 5–10 parts water. Before applying the paint, test the colour in a hidden area. Add water or paint as necessary, then apply with the synthetic sponge.

2 Once the wash is dry, spray the adhesive on the back of the stencil and position it (see pages 28–29). Apply the paint (see pages 30–31). Some paint will be absorbed by the wood, allowing the grain to show through.

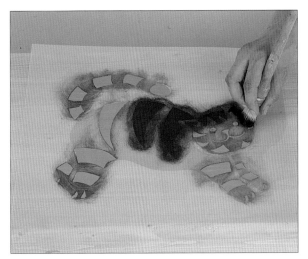

3 Once the stencil for the box top is completed in the first colour and is dry, remove the stencil, attach the second colour stencil and apply the paint through the cut-out shapes of this stencil. Continue until all colours are complete.

4 Once the stencilling is finished and dry, brush on two coats of water-based varnish. Finally add a little furniture wax applied with fine grade steel wool, then buff up with a soft, lint-free cloth.

## MELAMINE CUPBOARD

1 If the surface is poor, first apply a coat of water- or oil-based paint to match the original colour. To clean a surface in good condition, wipe over with a cloth wrung out in a solution of washing-up liquid.

2 Work out the position for the design, mark the stencil positions and attach the stencil (see pages 28–29). Mix the paint and apply it using the stippling method (see Stencilling Techniques, page 31). Build up the colour with further applications of paint.

3 Once the stencil design is complete and dry, varnish the design only. To do this, reposition the stencil carefully and apply water-based varnish through the stencil (see Protecting your Work, page 33).

# Fabrics

Natural fibres like cotton and linen, or a cotton and polyester mix, are the most suitable textiles for stencilling. Although fabric can be stencilled with almost any type of paint, if you are going to wash it use fabric paint which should be heat cured with a hot iron.

Fabric absorbs paint in a way in which walls or painted furniture don't, and so colours usually appear softer. Before decorating, wash fabric to remove any dressing and iron it well. It is also important to do a test to check how the colours will appear on the fabric and to make sure the colours won't bleed. Once you are satisfied with the colours and are sure that they will not run, you are ready to start on the fabric to be decorated.

**TOOLS:** Stencil, pins, soft-bristled stencil brushes

**MATERIALS:** Fabric, protective plastic sheet, masking tape, spray adhesive, water-based stencil or fabric paints, palette

(For safe use of spray adhesive see page 18.)

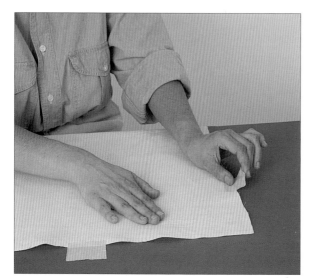

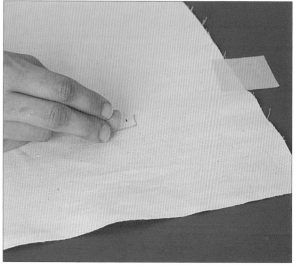

1 Lay out the clean, dry and ironed fabric on top of a sheet of plastic on a smooth surface – a plastic-coated table top is best. Using masking tape, tape a small piece of fabric to the table to hold it rigid. Large pieces of heavier fabric simply need weighting to stop them slipping.

2 Use pins or dressmaker's chalk to mark the positions for the stencil on the fabric.

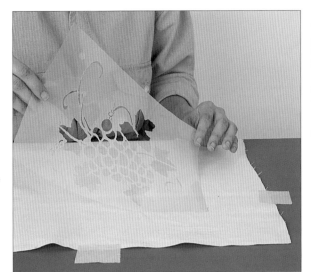

3 Spray the back of the stencil with the adhesive (see pages 28–29), and carefully lay the stencil in position, following marked guidelines and ensuring the fabric is flat beneath it. Remove and reposition if necessary, as creases can cause an irregularly coloured finish to the painted design.

4 A soft-bristled brush is essential, as its use ensures that the paint is well worked into the fibres. A domed brush is important for delicate shading. Pour out the paint, dip the brush into it and work the paint well into the bristles (see steps 2 and 3, pages 30–31).

5 Apply the paint with either a swirling or stippling action (see Stencilling Techniques, page 31). When the stencil is removed, you will find that a close-woven fabric produces clearer colours, an open-weave fabric gives a more hazy result. If using fabric paint, iron following instructions.

### USING TOO MUCH PAINT
When stencilling clothing or ready-made furnishings, ensure that you protect the fabric underneath the area you work on to guard against colour bleeding. It is also important not to overload the brush with paint as this can cause bleeding (see pages 36–37).

# Fabric paints

Depending on the fabric item to be stencilled, and how it should be washed, specific paints should be applied. Use the chart below to pick the appropriate paint for your chosen soft furnishing. The photographs on the right hand page show you how the paint 'takes'.

## FABRICS, PAINTS TO USE AND AFTERCARE

| FABRIC TYPE | PAINT TO USE | AFTERCARE Fabric paint | AFTERCARE Stencil paint | AFTERCARE Oil-based paint/spray |
|---|---|---|---|---|
| **Cotton or polyester and cotton mixtures** | | | | |
| Table cloth | Fabric paint | Iron to cure Machine wash Lasts as long as fabric | | |
| Bed linen | Fabric, water-based stencil paint, satin finish oil-based paint | Iron to cure Machine wash Lasts as long as fabric | Hand wash 15–20 washes before fading | Hand wash 50–100 washes before fading |
| Curtains | Fabric, water-based stencil paint, satin finish oil-based paint | Iron to cure Machine wash Lasts as long as fabric | Hand wash 15–20 washes before fading | Hand wash 50–100 washes before fading |
| Cushion covers | Fabric, water-based stencil paint, satin finish oil-based paint | Iron to cure Machine wash Lasts as long as fabric | Hand wash 15–20 washes before fading | Hand wash 50–100 washes before fading |
| **Muslin** | Fabric, water-based stencil paint, satin finish oil-based paint | Iron to cure Machine wash Lasts as long as fabric | Hand wash 15–20 washes before fading | Hand wash 50–100 washes before fading |
| **Silk** | Silk paints are best | Cure as recommended Hand wash | | |
| **T-shirt material** | Fabric, water-based stencil paint, satin finish oil-based paint | Iron to cure Machine wash Lasts as long as fabric | Hand wash 15–20 washes before fading | Hand wash 50–100 washes before fading |
| **Lampshades** Cotton | Fabric, water-based stencil paint, satin finish oil-based paint | Sponge clean with detergent solution when necessary | Sponge clean with detergent solution when necessary | Sponge clean with detergent solution when necessary |
| Card | Water-based stencil paint, oil crayons, satin finish oil-based paint, sprays | | Dust as required | Dust as required |
| **Roller blind** | Water-based stencil paint, oil crayons, satin finish oil-based paint, sprays | | Dust as required | Dust as required |
| **Shower curtain** | Water-based stencil paint, oil crayons, satin finish oil-based paint, sprays | | Wash carefully | Wash carefully |

# Stencilled fabrics

Different fabrics have varying levels of absorbency, are closely or loosely woven, with different textures. Absorbency, weave and texture can significantly affect the appearance of the stencilled paint. The examples below show some of these differences. Always do a sample first to check the effect.

**COARSE FABRIC    CHINTZ**

**WHITE CURTAIN FABRIC**

**CREAM CURTAIN FABRIC**

**WHITE MUSLIN**

**CREAM MUSLIN**

**CALICO**

# Tiles

Tiles are generally installed in hard-wear areas which need regular cleaning, like kitchens and bathrooms. These are also often steamy. The paint used for stencilling tiles in these areas must therefore be able to withstand such tough conditions. Ceramic paints are the ideal choice. Use cold-cure ceramic paints which dry and become hard at room temperature: other ceramic paints need firing in a kiln before use. On matt tiles, an oil-based paint can be used satisfactorily, provided that the tiles are fixed in an area which has light use and rarely need cleaning.

(For safe use of spray adhesive see page 18.)

*Painting glazed tiles*
**TOOLS:** Stencil, soft stencil brush
**MATERIALS:** Spray adhesive, masking tape, ceramic paints, palette

*Painting matt tiles*
**TOOLS:** Stencil, soft stencil brush
**MATERIALS:** Spray adhesive, masking tape, oil-based stencil crayons, palette

## PAINTING GLAZED TILES

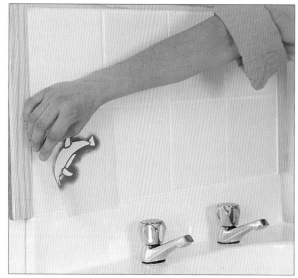

1 Clean tiles if necessary, spray adhesive over the back of the stencil and position (see pages 28–29). Add short lengths of masking tape to hold in place. If the stencilled design continues over grouting, apply water-based varnish through the stencil to seal the grout.

2 Using a gentle stippling action (see Stencilling Techniques, page 31) and a soft stencil brush, apply a small amount of cold cure ceramic paint. Gradually build up the colour in some areas to create shading but do this using the same colour paint: it takes too long to dry to add different colours to the same area.

**3** Take great care when removing the stencil as the paint smudges easily. Once stencilling is complete, allow the paints to dry and cure completely before use. This takes about two days.

## SOFT BRUSHES

Don't use hard bristled brushes to apply ceramic paints as bristle marks can clearly be seen.

## PAINTING MATT TILES

**1** Clean the tiles with a solution of washing-up liquid, then dry well. Spray adhesive over the back of the stencil and position carefully. Add short lengths of masking tape to hold in place if necessary (see pages 28–29).

**2** Prepare the paint from the stencil crayons (see steps 1–4, pages 32–33) and apply the paint with a gentle stippling action, building up the colour gradually. Add new colours, blending these with the first colour applied, to produce a soft, subtle effect.

**3** Remove the stencil with great care as paint will still be wet. Do not use the area for at least a day and preferably leave for three to four days for the paint to become completely hard.

# Projects

Many different surfaces and items can be stencilled using adaptations of the step-by-step techniques given already in this book. Although you may decide to decorate walls, floors, rugs, blinds, lampshades, a fire screen, glass and ceramic containers, all to match, you can overdo the effect.

Start by decorating just a few items and pick stencils designed on a theme, rather than using the same stencil repeatedly. Rooms where you relax, like living and bedrooms, can suffer from over stencilling, whereas you can happily go to town on areas you stay in for shorter periods like the hall, stairway, landing, bathroom and cloakroom.

And, once the house is stencilled, you can transfer your techniques to food decoration!

# Room frieze

In a room where a bold image is needed, use a large stencil and repeat this at intervals around the walls. Then combine these shapes with a co-ordinating pattern that forms a bridge between large designs, to create a wide frieze. This is a decorative way to cheer up a plain bathroom or line an otherwise empty staircase.

A large frieze can be used below dado rail height, at the top of a wall to lower the effect of a high ceiling, or to form a border to a large timber floor. Do a sample before you begin working on the surface to check the layout of the design and to choose the colour scheme.

(For safe use of spray adhesive see page 18.)

**TOOLS:** Large stencil, smaller stencil to join designs, chalk, stencil brushes

**MATERIALS:** Dust sheets, spray adhesive, masking tape, water-based stencil paint, palette

1 Take plenty of time to work out the area to be filled by the design. In a room with floor-standing fittings and furniture, first plan and mark the position where each large stencil design will go. The spaces between can be filled in with repeats of the smaller stencil.

2 Spray adhesive over the reverse of the main stencil and fix it in the first position. Use a dust sheet to protect the floor below and lay out the paints in readiness.

3 Apply the first colour (see pages 30–31) on all the areas of the stencil. A light tone is best used first, as it acts as a highlight and forms a good base for all the other colours. Here pale orange paint is used.

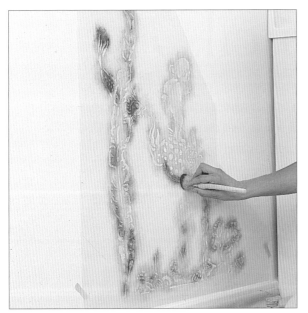

4 Add subsequent deeper colours for contrast and shading. Shade on top of your base colour by carefully building up darker layers of colour (see step 4, page 31).

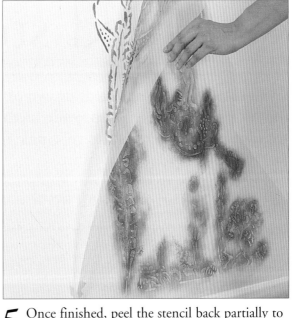

5 Once finished, peel the stencil back partially to check the effect. Re-colour any areas if necessary, remove the stencil and replace it in the second position and repeat as before.

6 With all the large stencils in place, add the smaller infill design. Use the same colours for both stencils. Where only partial sections of the stencil will fit the space, mask out the rest with masking tape.

7 Once stencilling is complete, remove the final stencil. Stand back to check you are happy with the effect and clean off any paint that may have marked door frames or skirtings.

# Grouped stencils

Use a single stencil, repeated, or two or three on the same theme and group them to provide pictorial areas on bare sections of wall. In this pattern, single fish are placed together to form shoals of fish.

    The best way to ensure you group stencils decoratively and choose the best colours is to do a sample first. Once you are happy with the arrangement and colours, you can start on the wall confident that the result will be just as you have envisaged it.

(For safe use of spray adhesive see page 18.)

**TOOLS:** Single stencil or stencils on a theme, stencil brushes, metal rule, step ladder if necessary

**MATERIALS:** Chalk, spray adhesive, masking tape, water-based stencil paint, palette

**1** Choose areas of blank wall for your design and mark the positions for each stencil in the group. Spray adhesive over the back of the first stencil and fix in the first position on the wall. Complete this stencil (see pages 30–31).

**2** Peel back the stencil and check the colours. Adjust if necessary. Replace the stencil to repaint the design in the second marked position, then any further positions, until the group design is complete.

3 Once the group is complete, compare the separate stencils and adjust if necessary.

## SOURCES OF INSPIRATION

When stencilling natural objects, look at illustrations and photographs for inspiration on where and how to shade the design.

## COLOUR APPLICATION

Do not be tempted to continue to add colour to a stencil or it could spoil the effect. Peel back the stencil, stand back to check the result and only then adjust if really necessary.

4 Here pictorial walls have been created by using stencils of the same style and theme to cover the area. Plan the main design before you start work. Once this is accomplished, stand back to check the overall effect and add extra sections where improvement is necessary. For further inspiration, look in the Ideas and Choices section on pages 6–13.

# Blinds and lampshades

Ready-made fabric articles in cotton and polyester can be stencilled with water-based stencil paints so long as they need washing only rarely. Stencilling is a simple way to enhance plain blinds, lampshades and curtains, including shower and net curtains. When stencilling over a dark-colour background, brush white stencil paint through the stencil cut-outs to block out the background colour. Apply subsequent colours over the top.

*Roller blind*
**TOOLS:** Stencils, soft stencil brushes

**MATERIALS:** Polythene dust sheet, spray adhesive, masking tape, water-based stencil paints, palette

*Lampshade*
**TOOLS:** Stencils, soft stencil brushes

**MATERIALS:** Polythene dust sheet, spray adhesive, masking tape, water-based stencil paints, palette

(For safe use of spray adhesive see page 18.)

## ROLLER BLIND

1 Lay the roller blind over the polythene sheet, flat on a table. If necessary remove any fittings, such as the batten at the blind base and the cord holder. Spray the back of the stencil with adhesive and carefully position, smoothing down well.

2 If the fabric colour is dark, first apply white stencil paint to the complete stencil design, using a swirling action (see Stencilling Techniques, page 31).

3 Once you have done this, peel back part of the stencil to check that all areas have been painted. When satisfied, leave for a few minutes to dry.

4 Paint the design. When the stencil is removed the colours applied over the white background show up well, including colours similar to that of the blind.

5 When completely dry, replace the batten and cord holder and hang the blind.

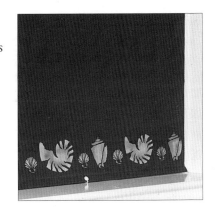

## LAMPSHADE

1 Spray the back of the stencil with adhesive and smooth onto the shade. Use strips of masking tape to hold each corner of the stencil in place. Stand back from the lampshade and check the stencil is positioned accurately.

2 With the soft brush and paint, apply the first colour using a swirling stroke. Use the brush almost dry and build up coats as highlights, using the stippling method (see Stencilling Techniques, page 31).

3 Once you have finished the first design and the paint is dry, position the second stencil and apply the paint for this in the same way.

4 This simple stencil design turns a plain lamp and shade into a colourful accessory that you can decorate to match or contrast with other furnishings in the room.

### SHADY PRACTICE

If you make a mistake when gauging where to place the design around a shade, so that the shapes are not equally spaced apart, alter your original design idea by adding extra elements from the stencils to hide the mistake.

# Rugs and mats

Apart from floors, natural fibre rugs and mats can also be stencilled. Spray paint is the best choice in this case because it sinks well into the fibres and won't loosen them – something which is difficult to accomplish with a brush.

(For safe use of spray adhesive and aerosol spray paints, see pages 18 and 21.)

*Cotton rug*
**TOOLS:** Stencils

**MATERIALS:** Spray adhesive, masking tape, lining paper or newspaper, aerosol spray paints, polythene dust sheet

*Coir mat*
**TOOLS:** Stencils

**MATERIALS:** Spray adhesive, masking tape, lining paper or newspaper, aerosol spray paints, polythene dust sheet, clear varnish

## COTTON RUG

1 Using a dustpan and clean brush, first brush the rug to ensure it is free of loose fibres. Vacuum to pick up any small stray fibres. Lay the rug out flat over the dust sheet, which protects the surface beneath.

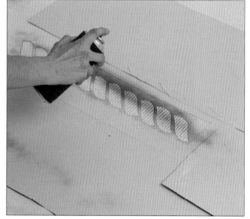

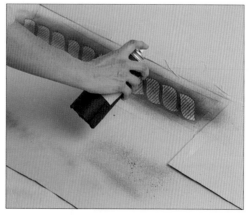

2 Plan the design and position the first stencil. Mask out the rest of the rug with lining paper taped to the stencil with masking tape (to avoid misting). Apply the first colour (see step 1, page 34).

3 Spray on your second colour as a highlight, building up the colour gradually (see steps 2–3, page 34). If the colour becomes too strong, apply a lighter shade of the same colour to soften it. Move the stencil and mask together to the second position.

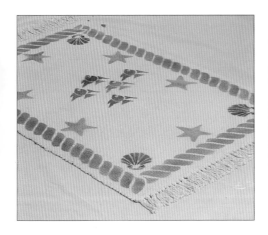

4 Once the border is finished and dry, apply the central motifs. The colours will gradually fade in time, but this has its own aged charm. See also the Brighten Up box, below.

## COIR MAT

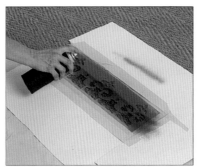

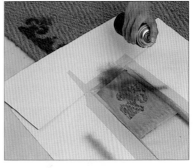

1 Ensure the mat is clean and free from loose fibres. Lay the mat on a plastic dust sheet on the floor or a table. Plan out the design, deciding how close to the edge the border should go. An ideal distance, on a mat of this size, is about 5cm (2in).

2 Spray the back of the stencil with adhesive and smooth down in first position. Mask an area around the stencil of at least 30cm (12in) on each side. Use masking tape to attach it to the stencil. Apply the first colour (see step 1, page 34), then the second.

3 Use an angled design stencil, as shown, to ensure a neat corner or mitre the design (see page 43). Use a light finger touch on the can and move it continuously. To ensure continuity keep colour depth the same on each area.

4 When you have finished the border, stand back and assess the result. If you need to make adjustments, follow the advice on pages 36–37, as appropriate. The mat is now ready for use.

# Fire screen

Medium Density Fibreboard (MDF) is an ideal material for a fire screen as it is easily shaped. Draw a template on paper for the main screen and a separate template for the feet and cut, or ask the timber merchant to cut the shapes for you. The main screen fits into a slot in the centre of each foot. Glue to fix. Choose a design to complement the screen shape and the style of the room. This screen was first emulsioned and then a coat of colour wash was added. Use a pale colour for the base coat and a stronger colour for the colour wash, so that it shows against the pale background.

(For safe use of spray adhesive see page 18.)

**TOOLS:** Household paintbrushes, synthetic sponge, stencil, stencil brushes

**MATERIALS:** Vinyl matt emulsion, fine sandpaper, water-based paint for colour washing, spray adhesive, masking tape, water-based stencil paint, palette, water-based clear varnish

1 Paint the screen with three coats of vinyl matt emulsion. Allow to dry and sand lightly between coats. Mix paint for colour washing. Dilute 1 part paint to 10–15 parts water. Check the colour on paper and add more water if necessary. Sponge on the colour wash.

2 Once the colour wash is dry, apply spray adhesive to the stencil and position it centrally on the screen. Apply the first colour (see pages 30–31). You may find it easier to lay the screen down flat, as in step 4, opposite. Work fairly quickly and carefully.

3 Add highlights and shadows (see step 4, page 31). Partially remove the stencil to check the result. If any alterations are required, reposition the stencil carefully and make the alterations (see pages 36–37). Remove the stencil.

4 If the design needs filling in, reposition the stencil to add extra flowers, leaves, or any other design element. Mask out the surrounding areas which are not to be included before you add paint to the newly positioned shapes.

5 Once complete, varnish the screen to protect it. Use two or three coats of water-based varnish, applied with a household paintbrush and according to the manufacturer's instructions.

**GUARANTEE THE RIGHT RESULT**
To ensure that you will be delighted with the result, check the design first. Using a sheet of paper, draw round the outline of the screen and cut out the shape. Stencil the complete colour design on the paper, cut it out and stick it to the front of the fire screen. Live with it for a few days and adjust if necessary.

# Containers

Glass or ceramic containers can be stencilled with most paints, but the surface soon wears off unless you use a cold-cure ceramic paint. This not only works well on bottles and pots, but can be used satisfactorily to decorate windows, mirrors and tiles as well.

(For safe use of spray adhesive see page 18.)

*Glass jar*
**TOOLS:** Stencils, soft stencil brush

**MATERIALS:** Container, spray adhesive, masking tape, card, cold-cure ceramic paints, polythene dust sheet, white spirit

*Terracotta pots*
**TOOLS:** Household paint-brush, stencils, soft stencil brushes

**MATERIALS:** Pots, pale household emulsion paint, spray adhesive, masking tape, water-based stencil paints, palette

## GLASS JAR

1 Thoroughly wash and dry the surface to be stencilled to remove all grease and dust. Spray the back of the stencil with adhesive and position as required. Use masking tape strips at the corners of the stencil to ensure it does not slip on the shiny surface.

2 Apply the first colour in ceramic paint, using the brush in a stippling action (see Stencilling Techniques, page 31) to achieve a soft, even result. Add the second colour almost immediately but take care not to smudge the paint. It is not practical to wait for the first coat to dry, as ceramic paints take 6 hours to touch dry and 3–4 days to harden completely.

3 Remove the stencil very carefully to avoid blurring the paint edges. If you are not happy with the result, remove the paint with white spirit, dry the surface well and repeat the stencilling. If a mistake can be easily rectified, leave the paint to dry and then make any alterations. (See also chart on pages 36–37.)

4 Use stencils on the same theme to match up a range of different-shaped bottles and jars. Wrap a stencil around a curved jar and fix with masking tape. Stencil each surface individually on containers with flat surfaces. Remember to take off the masking tape as soon as stencilling is complete, as it can bcome difficult to remove if left for a long time (see step 5, page 29).

## TERRACOTTA POTS AND SAUCERS

Cover a terracotta pot and its saucer with a coat of pale household emulsion. Then colour wash over this, as for the fire screen (see step 1, page 68), with a contrasting colour. When dry, decorate with a stencilled design, using the same technique as for the glass jar. Fix the paint by finally brushing on a coat of water-based varnish to all the pot's surfaces.

### WALL CUPBOARD

On a glass-fronted cupboard or door, create the look of etched glass. Fix a reverse cut-out shape (the area in a stencil that is normally removed) on the inside of the glass, sticking it in place with spray adhesive. Then, using white oil-based undercoat, stipple the glass on the inside (see Stencilling Techniques, page 31). When the reverse cut-out shape is removed this area appears as a transparent window.

# Cakes

Even a cake can be decorated with a stencil design! Use edible food colouring, available in both liquid and powder form. Here the powder form is used, mixed with water to form a thick liquid, and applied over royal icing. If you use liquid food colouring, take great care not to overload the brush: wipe it over kitchen paper so that the brush is nearly dry when the colouring is applied.

**TOOLS:** Stencils, small, soft stencil brush

**MATERIALS:** Syrup solution (optional, as it can tint the icing), liquid food colouring, palette, greaseproof paper

1 Place the cake to be decorated on greaseproof paper, on a flat surface. As spray adhesive cannot be used to hold the stencil in place, use a thin application of syrup solution instead, or hold the stencil down with your hand.

2 Apply the food colourings with an almost dry, soft brush and paint them on using the swirling technique (see Stencilling Techniques, page 31).

3 Once the design on the cake top is complete, remove the stencil carefully. Allow the colouring to dry before going on to the next stage.

4 Work out the spacing required between each stencil for the sides. Keep the cake at a slight angle while you apply the design. Hold the stencil and cake in one hand, while applying the colouring with the brush in the other hand. Move stencil and cake round as you work. Once complete, leave to dry.

5 Decorate the cake with bows, balls and ribbons or simply leave it stencilled, as desired. It is now ready to eat.

## ALTERNATIVE CAKE DESIGNS

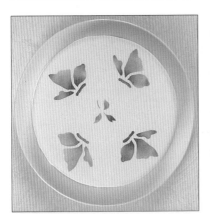

### Naturally attractive

For an enthusiastic naturalist, use stencilled butterflies, flowers, leaf patterns or other motifs from nature surrounding a central sprig.

### Dog day decor

Make a cake for a pet lover using a stencil design of their own breed of dog, cat or other animal, and complete with bows.

### DECORATING IDEAS

There are a number of different ways of decorating a cake using stencils. You can build up a 3-dimensional design by stencilling icing which has been rolled flat. Cut out the shapes and use syrup solution to stick them onto the top of a cake with plain icing. Alternatively, use a blitzer (see page 23) and food colouring felt tips to decorate a cake.

# Creating Illusions

Apart from decorating walls with borders, friezes and grouped motifs, you can build up a complete wall design or create illusions by stencilling items on the wall that you would like to include in the room but do not have the space, or the cash, to do so.

Trompe l'oeil designs are deliberately used to deceive the eye with life-like images. They allow you to include dream views of vast palatial gardens, antique furniture, wildlife, pets or anything else that appeals to you or to your sense of humour.

# Plate shelf

In a confined space, such as a small lobby, narrow kitchen, or landing, there is little room for furniture or wall-hung ornaments. This is an ideal place for a trompe l'oeil effect.

Stencil a shelf holding a decorative collection of glass or ceramics on the wall, create a group of wall-hung plates or add a painted dresser complete with a set of matching china. All these and many other effects can be created with stencils.

(For safe use of spray adhesive see page 18.)

**TOOLS:** Steel rule, spirit level, chalk, stencils, stencil brushes, step ladder

**MATERIALS:** Dust sheets, spray adhesive, masking tape, water-based stencil paint, palette

1 Use the rule, spirit level and chalk to mark the position for the shelf. Cut a simple shelf-shaped stencil making the shelf about 5cm (2in) deep and add short brackets about 10cm (4in) in from each end for a shelf as shown here (for Designing and Cutting Stencils see pages 82–91). The shelf on this wall is about 1m (3ft) long, for a longer shelf, add a middle bracket.

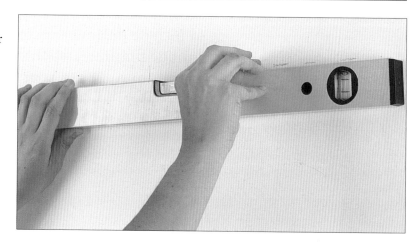

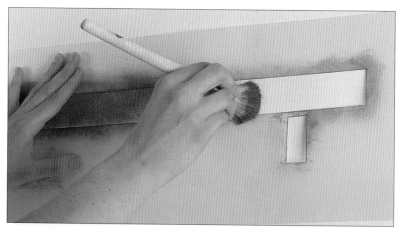

2 Here the shelf is stencilled in brown, using a sweeping action that imitates wood grain. Alternatively colour the shelf to match other items in the room. You could position shelving all around the room. For a very short shelf decrease the width of the shelf and the length of the brackets. Look at the shelves and brackets you already have for realistic lengths and widths.

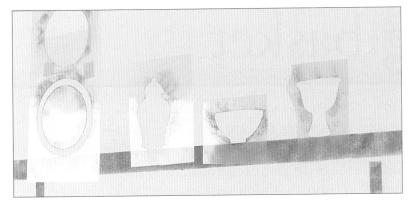

**3** Once you have finished the shelf and brackets fix the stencils in position for the plates, bowls and glasses you would like to 'display' along the shelf. Group some close together or space them out along the shelf.

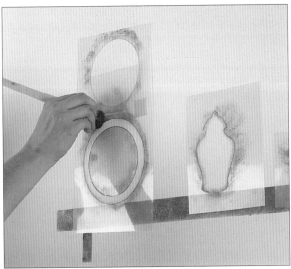

**4** The outer edge of a plate is stencilled as a faint shadow of blue, applied with an almost dry brush. Brush in a circle on the stencil allowing only part of the brush to touch the wall to give the effect of a plate rim, seen in step 5.

**5** Add the central plate design of your choice as a second stencil, applying it with a brush (see page 31). Complete the crockery set, adding shade at edges as in step 4. Designs can match to create a set, or be mixed for variety.

**6** The resulting stencilled design gives an impression of a collection of ceramics standing on a shelf. For an even more realistic result, spend time creating the effect of light and shade falling on the shelf and its contents (see step 4, page 31).

# Hanging basket

The main disadvantage of a real hanging basket is that it needs watering very regularly, and it requires replanting seasonally. Lack of care can result in pests or dying plants. Stencil your containers instead, indoors or in an outhouse, and fill them with the plants of your choice which will flower constantly and need no further attention!

(For safe use of spray adhesive see page 18.)

**TOOLS:** Steel rule, spirit level, chalk, stencils, natural sea sponge, stencil brushes, step ladder

**MATERIALS:** Dust sheets, spray adhesive, masking tape, water-based stencil paints, palette, plate

1 Chalk in a horizontal line to mark the position of the top of the basket liner. Check accuracy with the spirit level then spray the back of the liner stencil and press it to the wall. From the centre of the liner top mark a vertical line to the point where the hanging wires will meet.

2 Stencil the basket liner shape using a natural sea sponge and a gentle dabbing action, apply greens, browns and a little pale orange to imitate moss (see steps 1–3, page 35).

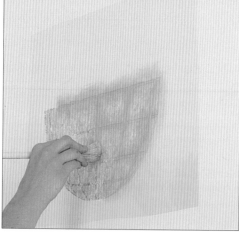

3 Use a second stencil positioned over the first for the wires of the basket. So that the wires show clearly, use a contrasting shade or a totally different colour. Green is used here but black would be a good alternative.

4 The hanging wires fall from the top of the central vertical line to join the basket at each side. Use a colour to match the wire basket and apply paint with the stencil brush.

5 Fix the plant stencil in place and use white paint to obliterate areas where the leaves will appear over the basket (see steps 2–3, page 64). Allow the white paint to dry.

6 Apply the true colours for the leaves. Build up colours to imitate the real leaves. Add further leaves as required using sections of the existing stencil and masking out areas that you do not wish to include. Leave to dry.

### IVY LEAGUE

Later, you could add to the design with extra climbing and trailing ivy, or add extra plants behind – gauge what will work best with your initial design. Let additional ivy strands wind up the hanging wires and trail further down the basket sides.

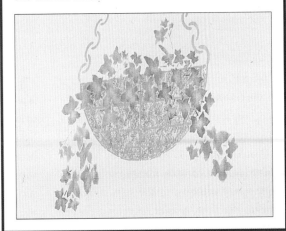

# Garden balustrade

If a room lacks an interesting view, why not use stencilling to transform a wall with the view of your choice. Here an ornate stone balustrade is topped with ivy-filled decorative urns. Once you have started, you can use stencils to create the garden of your dreams, be it a formal rose or herb garden, hedges decorated in topiary style, a lake or river abundant with birds and leaping fish. The simple design here would work well in a long corridor, or transform an otherwise bare concrete wall.

(For safe use of spray adhesive see page 18.)

**TOOLS:** Steel rule, spirit level, chalk, stencil, natural sea sponge, stencil brushes

**MATERIALS:** Dust sheets, spray adhesive, masking tape, water-based stencil paints, palette, plate

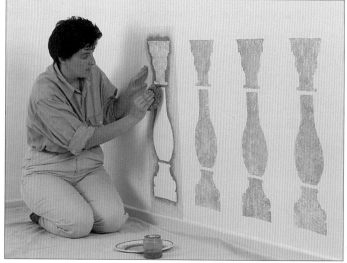

1 Work out the distance apart you want the balustrade uprights and the urns placed on the top rail, so that they fit neatly into the wall space available. Mark positions with chalk. Allow room for a balustrade base directly above the skirting. Apply spray adhesive to the stencil, and position the first upright, checking that it is vertical using the spirit level.

2 Use the sea sponge to apply the stencil paint with a gentle dabbing action (see steps 1–3, page 35). This imitates the texture of stone when viewed from a distance. Sponge brown over yellow paint to imitate sandstone, or brown over grey paint for York stone. You can use green in some areas for lichen. Work out the angle of an imaginery sun, and include the light and shade it would throw on the scene.

3 Once all the uprights are complete, the top and bottom rails can be added. Lightly chalk in two parallel lines the width of each rail, and fix detacked masking tape (see step 5, page 29) along the outside of each line. Sponge the rails in the same way as the uprights. Remove tape as soon as possible.

4 Once the paint on the top rail is dry, position the first urn and sponge this to match the balustrade. Add light and shade (see step 4, page 31) in the same way as on uprights. Repeat for all the urns.

5 Add ivy or flowers of your choice to go with the room's colour scheme. Where greenery or flowers trail over the container, stencil in white first to obliterate the urn colour, then stencil final colours.

6 The completed balustrade and urns may provide the right decoration for the room. Alternatively consider adding birds and insects like butterflies, ladybirds and bees or even a caterpillar, for fun. Later you could include a distant view, stencilled in pale receding colours, to give perspective.

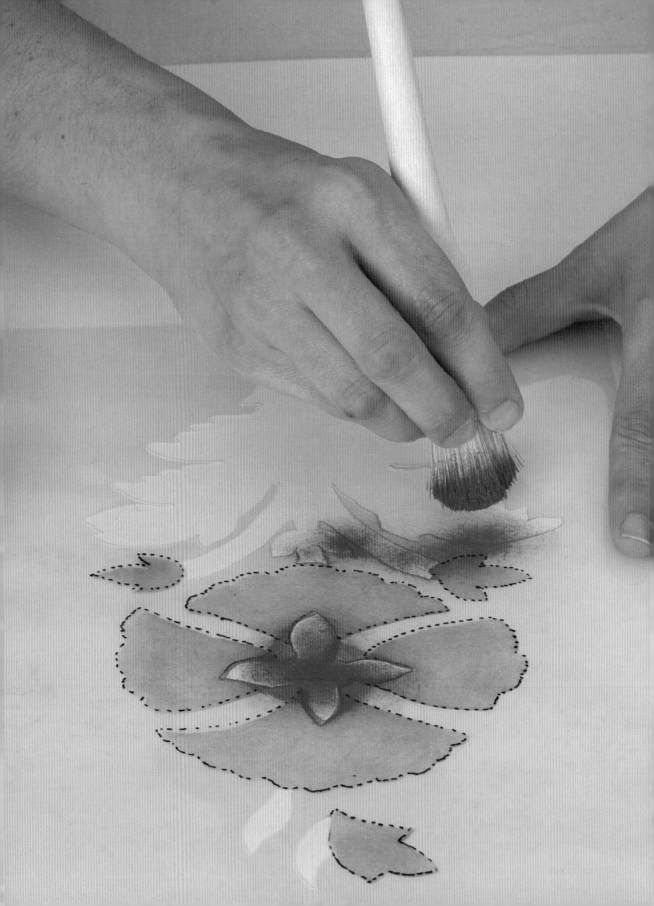

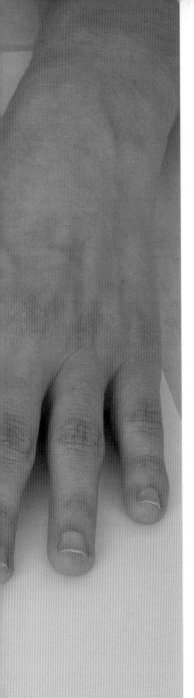

# Designing and Cutting Stencils

Bought stencil designs are limited and limiting. Once you have perfected your stencilling technique you will almost certainly wish to widen the source of material and this you can do almost limitlessly when you design and cut your own stencils. Not only are home-made stencils very cheap, but they are also individual to you.

You do not have to be artistic to design your own stencils: you can match up designs to the fabric in a room, use photographs and illustrations as a source, or copy from nature.

Stencils are designed in three ways: single layer stencils have all the colours and shapes on one stencil, outlined and divided by narrow bridges of stencil material; multiple layer stencils have a separate sheet for each colour; and detailing stencils are used to add intricate detail to a design.

# Single layer stencils

On single layer stencils the complete design, including any detail, appears on one sheet. If you cut all the way round an object the middle will drop out. Because divisions have to be made between colours and shapes, single layer stencils have thin connecting strips of stencil material known as bridges. These bridges give the finished result a distinctive stencilled effect and also help to stop the stencil becoming distorted in use. The most difficult part of creating a single layer stencil is deciding where to place these bridges. Looking carefully at the structure of a ready-made stencil will help you decide where bridges should go.

If you are producing an original design, plan your design carefully on a separate piece of paper. At first you may find it also helps to colour in your design. An outline of a shape or a colour is usually defined by a bridge, which may also be used to add detail in the form of the veins of a leaf for instance.

**TOOLS:** Fabric piece, solvent-based waterproof pen, stencil brush

**MATERIALS:** Tracing paper, stencil material, water-based stencil paint

1 Enlarge or reduce your original design on a photocopier until it is the correct size. Photocopying also helps to highlight the shadows, which is where bridges should appear.

2 Position a sheet of tracing paper over the design and trace the design on to it. First use the divisions between colours to form bridges. Bridges should be no less than 1.5mm (¹⁄₁₆in) when used to divide intricate designs and wider on bolder shapes.

3 Next look at areas within colours where shadows fall and use these for further bridges as necessary. Shade the areas to be cut out to check that one area does not bleed into another, and that the stencil will not fall apart.

4 Trace the design onto the stencil material to be used, and cut out the stencil. (See pages 88–91 for instructions on cutting out the different types of stencil material.) If at this point a mistake has been made and a vital part of the stencil has been removed, add this as a detailing stencil (see page 87).

5 Test out the finished effect by doing a sample on paper. Compare the finished stencil with the fabric pattern and make any alterations if necessary. The stencil is now ready for use.

## BUILDING BRIDGES

Bridges should appear at fairly regular intervals to keep your design intact.

To practise placing bridges, draw out and cut a simple design in different ways to find the best positions for them. It is worth spending time getting the design right at this stage.

Bold designs need fewer but wider bridges than intricate shapes. Use the contours of a design as bridges to highlight the shape, such as the veins of a leaf or divisions between the petals of a flower.

# Multiple layer stencils

Multiple layer stencils usually comprise a separate layer for each colour appearing in the stencil. This type of stencil does not require the use of bridges to divide areas but it is important to be able to line up each stencil accurately so that the various colours and shapes on each sheet appear in corresponding positions.

    This is done by using a dotted line to outline all the other shapes appearing on other stencils, together with the cut-out shapes on the one in use. Then, when the stencil is positioned, the dotted line outlines are matched up to the sections of the design which have already been stencilled and new colour is applied through the cut-outs. A detailing stencil is placed over an already stencilled area, to add intricate shapes to the design.

**TOOLS:** Fabric piece, solvent-based waterproof pen, stencil brush

**MATERIALS:** Stencil material, tracing paper, water-based stencil paint

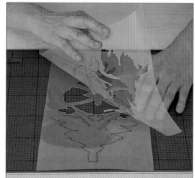

1 When using a design taken from a piece of fabric, enlarge or reduce the pattern area on a photocopier until it is the correct size. Colour in the design, as a separate stencil sheet is required for each colour shown. With very complicated designs this can mean up to ten different stencils.

2 Onto each sheet of stencil material trace the complete design. Use a dotted line for all the shapes not to be cut out, and a solid line for those shapes to be cut out. The continuous lines will appear on different sections on each stencil sheet. Cut out the solid lines (see pages 88–91).

3 Position and apply paint through the cut-outs on one stencil (see pages 30–35) in the first colour.

4 Apply the second colour through the cut-out shapes in the second stencil in the same way, ensuring that you line up dotted lines with the first colour outlines. Repeat for any further colours.

## DETAILING STENCIL

1 Add any delicate details on a separate stencil. Again, mark in the main outline with a dotted line, and the detail shapes with a solid line. Cut out, following the solid line outlines.

2 Carefully line up the detail sheet over the main stencil where colours have already been applied.

3 Add details using a darker or lighter shade of the original colour so that they are clear or choose different colours as a complete contrast.

4 Highly sophisticated and intricate effects can be produced using a number of overlays and one or more separate colour stencils.

5 This design shows grades of intricacy that can be included with a detailing stencil.

# Using a craft knife

When using a craft knife to cut either polyester or oiled stencil card, the knife needs even pressure and careful control, as it can easily slip. Use the knife in one long, continuous movement and move the stencil around as you follow the shape to be cut out.

Although a vinyl tile or even a magazine can be used as a base for cutting, a special cutting mat makes the job much easier as it helps to restrain and control the knife.

**TOOLS:** Craft knife, resealable cutting mat, solvent-based waterproof pen

**MATERIALS:** Stencil design, stencil material

## CUTTING STENCIL CARD

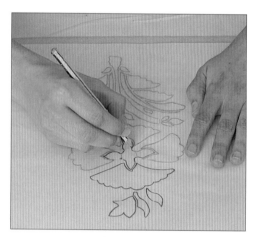

1 Transfer the design onto the stencil material using a reverse tracing technique. First trace the design onto tracing paper. Then place the 'drawn side' down on top of the manila card, and use a pencil to go over the design.

2 Go over the pale outline with the pen to make the design clearer. Compare with design on fabric.

3 Place the stencil on top of the cutting mat. Holding the knife in one hand, as you would a pencil, use the other hand to control the stencil. Pierce the stencil material and move the stencil around so that you cut in long, smooth, continuous sweeps, always working towards yourself.

4 Flick away a cut-out shape as you finish working around it. If you inadvertently cut through a bridge, mend the stencil (see page 25).

## CUTTING SURFACES

As a cutting surface, a resealable cutting mat is expensive but invaluable if you intend making a lot of stencils.

Alternatively use a thick, old magazine or a vinyl tile, but either of these surfaces should only be used once.

## CUTTING TRANSPARENT POLYESTER

1 In this case trace the design directly onto the transparent polyester. Place the stencil sheet over the design and draw in the lines with the solvent-based permanent pen.

## HOT KNIFE CUTTERS

By far the easiest method of cutting transparent polyester is to use a hot knife stencil cutter (see pages 90–91).

This melts the material and is similar to using a pen, but slower. It requires little effort, controlling the tip is not difficult, it is practically mistake free, and therefore enjoyable to use.

2 Use a hot knife cutter if you have one, or use the craft knife in the same way as when cutting card (see step 3, opposite). Once more a cutting mat offers much greater control, and so reduces the likelihood of mistakes.

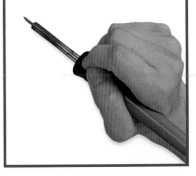

# Using a hot knife cutter

The hot knife stencil cutter has revolutionized cutting polyester and acetate stencils. The cutter has a hot tip which melts the material as it glides over it and it requires little effort to control it, whereas a craft knife needs a certain amount of strong pressure and very careful control. To protect the surface underneath the stencil when using a hot knife cutter, place a sheet of glass beneath the stencil.

**TOOLS:** Polyester or acetate stencil material, hot knife stencil cutter

**MATERIALS:** Sheet of polished-edge plate glass larger than the stencil

1 Using a solvent-based permanent pen, copy the design onto the polyester or acetate. Place the stencil sheet over the glass. You may find it useful to place the source design under the glass as well, to act as a reference.

2 Practise on a spare piece of stencil material first, then cut the stencil. Hold the hot knife stencil cutter upright by the handle, with the side of your hand resting on the cutting surface. This helps to keep your hand steady. Gently and slowly, cut through the stencil material in clean sweeps. If the knife skids you are going over the surface too fast, so slow down. A skid does not, however, damage the stencil, and cutting errors are unlikely.

3 On peeling back the transparent polyester the cut-out pieces are shown stuck to the glass and the stencil is cleanly cut out and ready to use.

4 When this cutter is used the cut-out shapes appear similar to those cut with a craft knife, but there is a fine ridge around the cut edge where the transparent polyester has melted. Excessive build-up of this ridge is due to holding the cutter at too much of a slant. However, this build-up does not impair stencilling; in fact in some cases it strengthens the stencil design.

## CUTTING STENCILS FROM ORIGINALS

Once you become adept at cutting using this technique, you can cut a design directly from an original by placing the source below the sheet of plate glass.

Make sure that you work directly above the design, or you may get some distortion through the thickness of the glass. Be especially careful to include bridges in single layer stencils. If you need to alter the design to include them, it is better to trace it and adjust your trace as necessary. Ink in the final design using a solvent-based permanent pen and proceed as outlined in the steps.

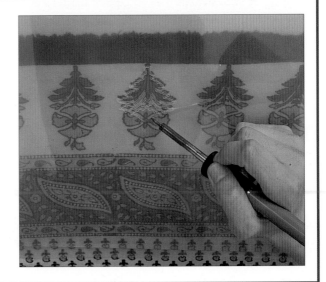

# Glossary

**Absorbed**
Liquid soaked up by the surface being worked on.

**Aerosol**
A canister holds vapour as liquid under pressure and in stencilling some paints and re-positioning adhesive come as aerosols.

**Bleeding**
Paint that seeps under the edge of a stencil.

**Blitzer**
Hand-held tool, which when pressed emits paint blown from the end of a felt tip.

**Border**
Repeating band of stencils that can be positioned at any height and on almost any surface.

**Bridges**
Narrow strips between open areas of a stencil that hold it together.

**Build-up**
Paint that sometimes accumulates at the edges of stencils.

**Chalk line**
Line drawn onto the surface to help position the stencil accurately.

**Colour wash**
Thin coat of paint and water applied to create a subtle surface texture and colour.

**Cure**
Period of chemical change when paint hardens to provide a tough waterproof surface.

**Cut-outs**
Areas removed for application of paint when a stencil is cut.

**Detack**
Remove some stickiness from a surface. Masking tape should be applied to a clean fabric surface a number of times before it is applied to a wall or it can damage the wall surface when it is removed again.

**Dilute**
Thin the paint with a suitable solvent to make it less concentrated.

**Domed-end brush**
Stencil brush with bristles that are rounded at the working end.

**Frieze**
Similar to a border, a band of decoration usually applied horizontally to a wall.

**Guide marks**
Chalk or pencil marks that aid positioning a stencil correctly.

### Highlight
Additional light or dark colours added to stencil to create effect of natural lighting.

### Horizontal Parallel
Line level with the ground.

### Line-up
Make one stencil match the position of another.

### Mask
Apply protection around a stencil to prevent paint misting.

### Mitre
A diagonal join across the corner where two border pieces meet at right angles.

### Multiple-layer stencil
Where more that one stencil is used to produce a single design.

### Parallel
Two lines that always remain the same distance apart.

### Polyester
Strong, transparent stencil material.

### Re-positioning spray adhesive
Low-tack spray glue that allows for repositioning.

### Seepage
Paint leaks under stencil.

### Single-layer stencil
Where only one stencil is used to produce a complete design.

### Stippling
Stencilling method where paint is applied in an up and down pounding movement to produce textured results.

### Swirling
Stencilling method where paint is applied in a circular movement to produce, smooth and soft results.

### Template
Pattern used as a guide when cutting.

### Trompe l'oeil
Literally something that deceives the eye. A painted scene or effect that represents real life.

# Index

*The authors and publishers would like to thank the*
*following for their assistance in producing this book:*

Janice Frost and family, Jenny Martin, Marina Tzirka and the Greek Orthodox Church,
Stephanie and Kavan Hashemi Brown, The Allen Brothers of Birmingham,
James and Sandra Crow, Sue Cassels, Jackie Steadman, Alison and Mark Rowley,
Mrs Piper, Bill and Lorraine Graham, Jackie Gilbert

Jessica Earle

All the staff in our shops who have borne the extra burden
while we have been working on this book

For mail order and sales information contact: The Painted Finish, Unit 6,
Hatton Country World, Hatton, Warwick, England CV35 8XA

Editor: Jenny Plucknett
Sub-editor: Carolyn Pyrah
Designers: Pedro Prá-Lopez and
Frances Prá-Lopez,
(Kingfisher Design)
Frank Landamore

Managing Editor: Miranda Spicer
Art Director: Martin Lovelock

Photography: Debi Treloar

Illustrator: Fred van Deelen

Production Manager: Kevin Perrett
Set Builder: Nigel Tate

Paula Knott and Peter Knott have asserted their
right to be identified as the authors of this work.

First published 1996

Text, photographs and illustrations
© Haynes Publishing 1996

Published by: Haynes Publishing
Sparkford, Nr Yeovil, Somerset BA22 7JJ

British Library Cataloguing-in-Publication Data:
A catalogue record for this book is available from
the British Library

ISBN 1 85960 110 3

Printed in France by
Imprimerie Pollina, 85400 Luçon - n° 68975 - C